# Factory Ride

Joann –
Thanks so much
for your help!
Carolee 5/29/04

# Factory Ride

## by
## Carolee Tyson

www.lazerquick.com

Pumpkin Ridge Publishing
PO Box 1668
North Plains, OR 97133
(503)647-5970
PRPublish@msn.com

Front & Back Cover: Hunter White
Back Cover: Brooke White & Nathan Tyson

ISBN: 0-9754459-0-1
Library of Congress Control Number: 2004093563

Printed in the United States of America.

---

**How to Order**
Single copies may be purchased on the internet and
at your local bookstore. Quantity Discounts are
available for retail, schools and libraries. Contact
Pumpkin Ridge Publishing
PO Box 1668, North Plains, OR 97133
telephone (503)-647-5970
email PRPublish@msn.com

---

Visit us online at
**www.FactoryRide.com**

This book is dedicated
to my children and step-children,
whose young lives
are full of choices.

| CHAPTER | PAGE |
|---------|------|

## Chapter 1 – VISION

Twenty-five two-stroke 250cc motorcycles revved in anticipation at the starting gate. Their exhilarating growl made it impossible to hear anything else.

Inside a pair of motocross goggles, Austin's stern and serious eyes shifted nervously back and forth. A bead of sweat dripped through his thick brown eyebrow, across his temple and left a faint trail on his dusty cheek. The expression on Austin Davis' boyishly handsome face oozed both fear and adrenaline-pumped excitement.

This was the race he'd been waiting for his whole life.

Wearing brand new top-of-the-line motocross gear, Austin looked pensively to his right. He saw the usual army of racers wearing protective gear in a myriad of brilliant colors. He had known most of them since he was a little kid. They rode Honda's, Suzuki's, Kawasaki's, and Yamaha's. Only one other rider had a KTM, and he wasn't very good. Austin knew he had the edge. He dropped his head and closed his eyes, mentally psyching himself up. This was it.

"My choice. My way."

In what seemed like slow motion, Austin watched the starting gates drop, released the clutch then exploded away in first gear. Like a well-trained soldier in a platoon, Austin didn't skip a step. In a matter of seconds he kicked it into second gear, pulled in the clutch, hit the back brake, whipped out a sharp left turn, and made the holeshot. As the first rider out of the first turn, he jetted away from the pack acutely aware of his narrow lead. Another rider, dressed in all black gear, was right behind him. And Austin could feel it.

Oblivious to the wildly cheering crowd, Austin's attention was focused on the track as he screamed his bike through the first hairpin turn. From the corner of his goggles, he saw his roostertail spray the Black Rider. With renewed determination, Austin twisted the throttle and jetted off the berm. It was do or die. Neck and neck, Austin battled the unrecognizable competitor throughout the entire fast-paced and teeth-gritting two-mile race.

Ignoring his own exhaustion, Austin saw the checkered flags waving at the end of the gnarly whoops and kept up the brutal pace. Riding balls out and still gassing it, Austin's back tire only hit every third or fourth whoop, and his front wheel never touched the ground. But, the Black Rider was suddenly right beside him and gaining ground.

"C'mon!" Austin screamed at himself.

Engulfed in a fury of dust and noise, Austin didn't have time to react when the Black Rider got too close beside him. There was nothing he could do to prevent their handlebars from cracking into each other as they shot over the last whoop in unison.

The sudden jolt caused Austin's bike to instantly lose momentum. The front wheel slammed down onto the track, casing the front end and throwing the bike into a rapid endo. As a result, both riders were pitched from their bikes and sailed through the air like gunshot birds. Fifteen feet later, they landed in the dirt with a hard, sickening thud.

Face down on the ground with the wind knocked out of him, Austin rolled over and gasped desperately for one single breath. He looked up, eyes wild with fear, just in time to watch his bike slam down on top of him.

Austin jerked awake when the sound of his digital alarm clock suddenly mixed with the revving two-stroke engines in his dream. He threw back the worn blankets, leaped out of bed and swatted the irritating buzzer. The motocross magazine that was sprawled across his heaving chest dropped to the floor. Wearing ratty boxers and still breathing hard from his nightmare, Austin leaned against his old, scratched dresser and took a second to catch his breath and get a grip.

Austin's bedroom was tidy but small. Opposite the dresser and squeezed in between the wall and his sagging twin bed was a bookcase stuffed full of motorcycle repair manuals for every imaginable make and model of bike. Both the bookcase and the dresser were covered with dozens of motocross trophies, some big, some small. Posters of motocross bikes and racers hid the damaged and yellowed walls.

Austin forced open a stuck dresser drawer and pulled out a pair of Levi's. His physique was impressive. Pushing six foot, he was taller than the average motocross rider. And at almost eighteen years old, his young body was in prime physical condition. With virtually no body fat, his ripped and developed muscles were easily evident. Organized, confident and disciplined, he looked like a young GI Joe.

He quickly slipped into his jeans, pulled a Fox t-shirt over his head and ran his fingers through his short brown hair. He put on a pair of dingy white socks and stepped into worn out leather Redwing boots. Ready for school, Austin grabbed his faded backpack and headed for the kitchen.

Starving and in a hurry, Austin pulled a jug of milk out of the grimy avocado green refrigerator. He poured milk onto his generic Cheerios, took a bite then put the milk back. Still chewing, he opened the cabinet next to the fridge. It was completely empty.

"Damn."

Austin opened the cabinet under the sink and dug frantically through the trash. Finally, he found the empty vodka bottle he knew would be there. It was covered with coffee grounds so he quickly pulled it out and rinsed it off in the sink. He took another bite of cereal and glanced over his shoulder. Already mentally conditioned, he knew he didn't want to get caught.

He turned on the faucet and filled the bottle with water. More digging in the trash produced the lid. He wolfed down the rest of his cereal and put his bowl on top of a week's worth of dirty and smelly dishes already in he sink. He screwed on the lid, stuffed the bottle into his backpack and ran down the outside steps that led to the basement garage.

Austin dropped his backpack in the dirt and rolled open the old wooden garage door. The paint on the light blue house was almost gone. Like the hope of the man that owned it, it had slowly peeled away over the years. Rusty wheels on the track overhead whined in protest but, as always, were ignored. Austin followed a ray of sunshine into the dark and dingy space.

Just like the house, it had been years since it was cleaned and smelled exactly like a basement does - dank, musty and wet. Cobwebs hung from the exposed rough-cut wood beams. The tiny windows were too dirty to let light in, much less see through. Dusty boxes were piled high next to old paint cans and crates of miscellaneous junk. Near the bottom of the heap, old and dull trophies in a crushed cardboard box no longer reflected the sunlight and were barely visible. Austin didn't even know they existed.

He squinted into the dark, back corner of the garage and grinned. "There she is."

Glowing in the morning sun was his diamond in the rough - a beat-up, run-down KTM 250 dirtbike. Even though it was spotlessly clean, the ten-year-old motorcycle looked every bit its age. The seat was faded and torn and the handgrips were worn thin. The plastics, especially the orange shrouds, were gouged and chipped. Both black fenders were attached to the bike with baling wire and electrical tape. But the engine, the most important part, still had life in it.

Austin flipped a light switch. A fluorescent bulb flickered to life in the back corner and lit up a spotless workbench, an organized tool board and a swept clean concrete floor.

Remembering where he left off, Austin quickly took a wrench from an old tool cabinet and removed the top-end on his bike. Like a professional NASCAR mechanic in the middle of a race, he felt pressed for time.

Right on schedule, a horn honked outside. Austin quickly put the wrench back into the cabinet drawer, wiped his hands on a rag and grabbed his backpack. After shutting the garage door, he switched gears and casually sauntered up to the waiting pickup. The shiny, brand new, decked-out truck seemed out of place next to the rundown house.

Jack Preston, the handsome driver, looked every bit his upper-class lifestyle except for the obnoxious hoop earrings in both ears. Ben Wilson, another silver spoon, hung his tatt-covered arm out the passenger window and motioned for Austin to hurry up.

"You got my part?" Austin demanded.

"Yeah, I got the fricken part," Jack replied. "You got the bottle?"

"You first," Austin said.

Ben taunted a new piston and rings out the window at Austin and whined, "Here you go, poor boy."

"Shut up, asshole," Austin snapped back. "What I don't have in money, you don't have in balls!"

Ben jerked the piston back into the truck, dropped it onto the rich leather seat and flung the door open. "You wanna bet? Let's go!"

Austin grinned and shook his head. "You got a damn short memory don't you, Ben?" He stuffed the bottle back into his backpack then took a quick step toward the truck.

Jack reached across Ben and held him back. "Knock it off." He picked up the piston and handed it to Austin, "Here. Take it. "

With shaking hands, Ben quickly pulled the truck door closed as Austin forced the piston into his backpack next to the vodka bottle.

"How 'bout we race for it?" Austin asked Jack. "If I win, I keep the part and the booze. You win, it's two bottles for you." Austin paused, "but I still keep the part."

Jack laughed, "You gotta be kidding? You

know I can kick your butt on the track!

"No problem," Austin said. "My old man likes his vodka."

"Fine," Jack relented. "Sunday. My place."

"Sure," Austin nodded toward Ben. "But make sure your dog is tied up. I wouldn't want him to break his teeth chasing my back tire."

From behind the safety of the truck door, Ben took a swing at Austin through the window. Austin snapped back out of reach and threw Ben a challenging smirk. Just as Jack stomped on the accelerator, Austin motioned for Ben to bring it on. With Ben involved, racing on Sunday was sure to be hazardous.

## Chapter 2 – DETERMINATION

At home on another Saturday night, Austin sat at the kitchen table and ate box mac and cheese out of a large pan.

His dad, Steve, came home late again from work and dropped his metal lunchbox on the counter. He pulled a bottle of vodka in a brown paper bag out of the lunchbox and quickly made himself a drink. Austin didn't pay any attention. He had seen this routine a thousand times. In fact, he didn't remember not seeing it.

Steve's solid gold wristwatch shimmered as he filled a glass three-quarters full of vodka and added a splash of orange juice. The deep chiseled lines in his ruddy alcoholic complexion added a dimension of fear to his already tense demeanor and made him look all the more threatening.

Austin looked up at him and noticed the muscles in Steve's jaw tighten then relax. Tighten then relax. Without saying anything, Steve sat down at the marred table adjacent to Austin and took a long, slow drink.

Trying to avoid his dad's harsh and abusive edge, Austin picked at his food while he carefully chose his words and waited for the right moment to speak. Finally, he broke the silence. Austin spoke quietly and slowly.

"Okay if I go to Jack's on Sunday?"

There was a long pause.

"What for?" Steve finally asked.

"Uh, I got a wager goin' for parts." Austin braced himself. "A little race...that's all."

Steve's emotions exploded under his loosely controlled façade. He failed to suppress his anger and Austin saw the rage boiling in his bloodshot eyes.

"Forget it!" he barked. "It's a bad idea and you know it!"

Austin slowly reached out and nearly touched Steve's arm. Almost begging he said, "C'mon, Dad. It'll be fine."

Steve raised his voice and moved his arm away. "You know we don't have any medical insurance. I can't afford for you to get hurt. No! You're not racing!"

Austin jerked his hand back and slammed the pan down on the table.

"Well, how else am I supposed to get parts for my bike? There's no extra money for me in your wallet!"

"You got food, clothes and a roof over your head," Steve yelled. "What more do you want?"

Austin got up from the table and threw the pan into the filthy sink. Noodles flew out and stuck to the wall. He knew it wasn't a question, but answered it anyway. "A decent life! Hell, it's no wonder Mom left you!"

In one movement, Steve leaped from his chair, grabbed Austin around the neck and slammed him up against the green refrigerator.

With his feet dangling and his toes barely touching the floor, Austin gasped for a breath as the back of the old wooden chair bounced off the ripped linoleum floor.

Steve's gold wristwatch shimmered as he held Austin by the throat and glared at him in eerie silence. The muscles in Steve's face twitched. His eyes blinked rapidly, his nostrils flared, and something inside him snapped.

At the top of his voice Steve yelled at Austin, "She left you too, you little son-of-a-bitch! And don't you ever forget it!"

Austin was running out of air. As soon as he felt Steve's grip loosen ever so slightly, Austin quickly jerked himself free and made his escape. On his way out of the kitchen he muttered under his breath, "Like you'd let me forget it."

Needing his own space and looking for isolation, Austin retreated to the basement shop to work on his bike and forget the reality of his world. He turned the radio on to his favorite station. When a Creed song came on, he instinctively reached over to turn up the volume, but then decided against it. No sense upsetting the old man even more.

Upstairs, Steve fixed another drink and leaned against the kitchen counter. Looking like he just came from a funeral, he stared blankly into the dark living room. He took a long, slow drink of his screwdriver and tried once again to drown the pain inside. His eyes teared up, but he gritted his teeth, took another drink and pushed the old emotions back down.

Down in his basement shop, Austin wrapped a rag around his new piston, put it into the vise and gingerly clamped it down. He took a ring compressor and put on the new rings. He removed the piston from the vise, held it up to the light and inspected his work. He noticed Steve standing in the doorway, but kept on working. Screw him.

Steve, holding a full drink, leaned against the doorjamb and watched him for a moment before breaking the silence. "Look, I know you think you got it bad around here, but it could be worse," Steve said.

Austin threw him a daggered look and kept working.

"I know. I used to be just like you when I was your age," Steve continued. "I loved motorcycles."

"You'd never know it now," Austin said.

"I got on with my life. Nobody I knew then...or now...makes a living racin' bikes," Steve snorted.

"Well, it's what I want to do." Austin used an old rubber hammer to gently tap the piston into the cylinder. "And I could be so much better if I had the right tools."

"You know the odds," Steve replied. "Getting a Factory Ride is like making the Olympic team."

"There you go again," Austin snapped back, "the Dream Crusher."

Steve gestured wildly with his hands as he talked. "You know I can't afford a new bike and all that fancy gear."

Austin glared at his dad's sloshing drink and knew the alcohol must have kicked in. "You manage to afford plenty of orange juice," Austin mumbled to himself.

"Why don't you play football or baseball?" Steve asked, oblivious to Austin's remark.

"This is my last year in school, Dad. I gotta decide what I'm gonna do with my life."

"Get a job," Steve replied flatly.

"Yeah," Austin replied, "and end up working for peanuts the rest of my life. I could be just like you."

"You watch your damn mouth!" Steve barked. "Just because you're gonna finish high school doesn't make you any better than me. You got more options, that's all!"

Austin refused to back down. "Racing motorcycles. That's my option. It's what I'm good at."

"You're also good at welding. I'll get you a job down at the shop," Steve slurred.

Austin shook his head. He wasn't buying it. No matter what, he refused to end up like his dad.

"I'd rather stick to bikes," he said calmly. "They're my ride outta here."

Steve reacted and fired back, "Yeah?

Where the hell you think you're gonna end up?"

Austin stopped working and looked blankly at his father.

"I'll tell ya," Steve said. "Right back here!"

## Chapter 3 – FRIENDSHIP

In the early Sunday morning light, Austin tiptoed through the dark living room past Steve, who was still asleep on the couch. The couch was the only thing in the house that wasn't old or worn out, but it embarrassed Austin that it came from the neighbor's garage sale.

Austin quietly opened the door to the basement shop. Just before he went down the steps, he glanced quickly back at his father. He was still holding his glass in one hand and the empty bottle in the other. Must have been another one of those nights.

In the basement, Austin folded his Levi's around his calf and tried to force his foot into his old motocross boot. He cringed as he stepped down. "Damn!" He pulled off the too-small boot and flung it hard against the concrete block wall. He laced his Redwings back up and buckled the strap of his beat-up helmet under his chin.

He took his bike off the stand and silently pushed it outside. "I hope this thing starts," he said to himself. He reached down and opened the fuel line, flipped down the kick-starter and gave it a swift kick. Austin grinned as he listened to it idle.

It sounded beautiful. To Austin, that gentle noise was like his own potential. He knew that with just one quick twist of the throttle and a little bit of fuel, the quiet put…put…put could be instantly transformed into raw power. Into success.

He clicked the bike into gear then putted as quietly as he could up the driveway. Once on the main road, he turned north and headed toward Jack's house and practice track. Shifting quickly through the gears, the faster Austin went, the freer he felt. The high pitched revving of the two-stroke engine left a trail of sound in the cool morning air that faded away behind him.

Back in the house, the noise from the bike woke Steve with a start. Hung over, he staggered to the front door and flung it open. Following the sound, he caught a glimpse of Austin screaming his bike up the road and cringed as Austin neared a stand of fir trees that grew off to one side.

Uncontrolled and without notice, Steve's flashback hit him like a ton of bricks. He grabbed onto the doorframe to steady himself as his memory played back like hazy, yellowed film footage. For an instant, a 1970's motocross racer that matched Austin's image exactly, sped recklessly away from him and headed toward a stand of fir trees that lined a motocross track.

---

At Jack's motocross track, a dozen riders

dressed in the latest motocross gear circled the track and practiced freestyle tricks. Austin shifted down and coasted to a stop next to Jack, who was decked out in all the latest apparel. Aside from his ratty helmet, Austin didn't own motocross gear. He couldn't afford it.

"I don't believe it. Look who showed up," Jack said.

"Thinkin' about pussin' out?" Austin challenged him with a grin.

"Yeah, right," Jack said.

Jack watched as Ben flew off the tabletop, executed a Superman, landed rough and kicked up a cloud of dust. Jack shook his head as Ben rode up beside him.

"What," Ben demanded.

"What kind of landing is that?" Jack laughed. "Shit! You ride like a chick!"

"I don't see you trying it," Ben fired back, who looked a little put out.

"Freestyle's your rush, not mine," said Jack.

"Think I can pull a backflip?" Ben asked.

"Not without a butt-load of practice," Jack answered skeptically.

"You bring the booze?" Jack asked Austin.

"Hell no. And that piston's already in," Austin smiled.

"Like that's gonna help you get that piece of shit over the tabletop," Ben sneered.

"Only one way to find out," Austin yelled as he pulled away.

Pumped with anticipation, Austin flew
onto the track. Riding with great form and an
edgy competitive angst, Austin didn't look like
he was riding a motorcycle - he looked like he
*was* the motorcycle. Using momentum and
gravity to his advantage, he kept his body
centered and used it to perfectly balance the
bike. And no matter what condition the terrain
or track was in, he kept his feet on the pegs
except in the most grueling of corners.

As Jack and Ben watched Austin from their
resting place alongside the track, another rider
on a TM 300 pulled up next to them and let off
the throttle. The TM idled like a purring tiger as
Gary, Jack's dad, removed his goggles and
helmet. Handsome and in good shape, he owned
Coast Range Cycle, a thriving motorcycle
business.

"Who is that?" he asked Jack. "I told you,
only people we know on the track! The business
doesn't need a lawsuit!"

"It's just Austin," Jack replied as he
watched Austin overshoot the corner and face
plant into the berm.

"Thinks he's good enough to get a Factory
Ride," Ben laughed. "Yeah, right."

Concerned for Austin's safety, Gary
nervously watched Austin right his bike on the
steep bank of dirt.

"Steve know he's up here?"

"Don't know," Jack answered.

"Well, find out," Gary demanded. "And get

him some goggles!

Gary got back on the track and rode like the pro he could have been. Gary sailed over jumps and chewed around corners like he was tethered to the inside.

Austin caught sight of Gary from across the track and pulled off the track to watch him. Gary's abilities were impressive. Austin hoped that someday he would be like him.

Later that morning, Ben waved all the riders off the track for the big race. Jack, riding a brand new Honda CR250, pulled his bike up next to Austin, who waited on the track's mock starting line and revved his engine. Austin looked over at Jack's bike. It was brand new. Everything was in pristine condition. Not even the plastics were scratched.

"Must be nice to have an old man that owns a motorcycle shop," Austin thought.

"The first one to finish five laps wins," Jack announced.

Jack looked at Austin and nodded, then flipped him off. Austin grinned and flipped him back. Since they were little boys, it had been their good luck signal.

Ben walked onto the track and stood in front of Jack and Austin. He nodded at Jack then dropped his arms. The race was on!

Austin matched Jack move for move, turn for turn until the uphill on the back straight. Using only half the meat the low-end had to offer, Jack twisted the throttle on his bike and pulled ahead, making it into the next curve ten lengths ahead of Austin.

When the ground leveled out, Austin rode the guts out of his KTM and headed for the tabletop. Sailing through the air, he landed dangerously close behind Jack then gassed it.

Austin cut Jack off in the corner and took the lead, only to lose it again on the uphill. Five laps later, Jack sailed over the mock finish line, with his hands raised in the air, past his cheering friends.

"Damn," Austin thought as he shook his head in defeat. "More booze."

A short while later Cindy, Gary's energetic wife and savvy business partner, walked up next to the track and sat an ice chest down in the grass. A cell phone balanced on top of it. She waved her arms and signaled to the riders. The riders, fifteen in all, pulled up together and got off their bikes. Cindy smiled at the symphony of Velcro as everyone peeled off their gloves.

One by one, the riders peeled off their helmets and hung them on the handlebars. Their faces were covered with dust and sweat except where their clean eyes had been protected  by goggles. Those clean eyes were all wild with excitement from the rush only racing released.

"Thanks, babe," Gary said as everyone dug into the ice chest for a soda.

"You're welcome, hon," Cindy said as she looked around at the grinning group of dusty young men. "You all look like a bunch of raccoons!" Cindy laughed. "Except Austin." Cindy smiled at him. She liked him.

Everyone turned to look at Austin, who hung at the back of the group. His face was completely covered with dust. Even the creases in his eyelids had dirt caked in them.

"I thought I told you to get him some goggles," Gary said to Jack.

"Sorry, Dad. I forgot," Jack apologized. "You like eating my dust, Austin?"

"This isn't your dust, Jack," Austin said. "It's my own. It doesn't have time to settle by the time I come around again."

"Yeah, right," Ben quipped. "Not on that piece of shit."

"You watch your mouth in front of my wife!" Gary snapped at Ben.

"Sorry, Gary," Ben mumbled.

"Your dad know you're up here?" Jack quickly asked, remembering his dad's question and wanting to avoid a public reprimand.

"Yeah, I told him."

"What'd he say?" Gary asked.

Cindy's cell phone rang. She flipped it open and answered it. "Hello?"

"That I should play football in the Olympics instead," Austin said as he shook his head at the ridiculous idea.

The kids in the group laughed. Most of them didn't know Steve or anything about Austin's difficult life. But they knew that they weren't jocks. They were motocross riders.

There was a big difference – they were better.

Austin quickly glanced at Gary. He wasn't laughing. From the serious expression on Gary's face, Austin realized that Gary knew more about his dad than he thought.

Cindy handed the phone to Gary. "It's for you. It's the shop."

Gary talked into the phone without attempting to keep the conversation private. The curious riders drank their sodas but paid attention to the call. They couldn't help it. Gary's life was fast-paced and interesting. He was their idol of sorts and an all around great guy to be around. Plus, he gave good deals on parts and equipment if you raced with his logo *and* he liked you.

"During the race at Washougal yesterday?" Gary listened intently. "Broke his femur in two places and cracked three ribs." Another pause. "Out for a least three months. Okay."

The riders looked at each other and cringed in unison as the accident flashed in their minds. In slow motion, they saw the rider go down on the red clay dirt. Their faces grimaced when they imagined the man's leg bones snapping as they twisted grotesquely around his bike.

"Aw sick! Wicked awful. That sucks," the riders groaned quietly after Gary snapped the phone shut. They all knew pain.

Cindy gave Gary a puzzled look.

"Dave. The new salesman. Man, that's gotta hurt. Especially at his age," Gary said. He tossed his top-of-the-line goggles to Austin. "Here, try these. And take Ben's bike." Gary glanced at Ben. "It will remind him to watch his mouth."

Ben groaned silently to himself but didn't visibly protest. He knew better.

"Double or nothing? Austin said to Jack.

"What you got?" Jack replied as he looked at Austin and nodded, casting a subtle sideways glance at Gary.

"I'm thinking about getting some new bars," Austin said. "These are three-fifths worn out."

"Now how do you measure that?" Gary laughed in disbelief.

"It's just a joke from physics class, Gary," Austin said smiling.

"Austin's a pretty bright boy, Dad," Jack interrupted, trying to keep their deal under wraps. "He's graduating with honors. Valedictorian or something like that."

Austin pulled on his helmet and started to slide Gary's goggles into place.

"That's great, but wash your face first," Gary said. "Those are my *new* goggles!"

Austin walked away from the group to the ice chest, opened the drain tab and rinsed his face. He pulled off his t-shirt and used it as a towel to dry his face. His sweaty, well-defined muscles rippled in the hot sun. Austin wiped his face and looked up at Ben, who was suddenly right next to him. Out of earshot from the others, Ben bent down and picked a blade of grass to put between his teeth and hissed, "You break my bike you buy it, needle-dick."

Used to Ben's hot air and cutting remarks, Austin ignored him and walked back to the group. He pulled on his t-shirt and helmet then slid Gary's goggles carefully into place. Jack started and revved his bike, eager to remind Austin again of the already established pecking order.

Austin threw a leg over Ben's new KTM SX250 and motored onto the track. He took the first lap slow so he could get used to the new bike. Man, it was powerful. As he passed the group, Jack followed him onto the track.

The group cheered and yelled, "Come on! Go Jack! Kick it up!" Without openly choosing sides, Gary and Cindy watched the drama play out.

Austin dropped the clutch, opened the throttle and charged up the face of the tabletop with Jack right beside him. They hit the tabletop together and soared through the air like twin jets.

"They have always been so competitive," Cindy said to Gary, who nodded his head in agreement.

Austin and Jack landed in perfect poetic unison. The group cheered. What a show! Finally on a decent machine, Austin opened up the throttle and attacked the course with the smoothness of McGrath and the tenacity of

Carmichael. To Gary's surprise, Jack struggled frantically to keep up with him. Throughout the entire race, Austin maintained his lead.

"Austin's that good?" Gary asked in disbelief loud enough for everyone to hear.

"Can't be," Ben replied not wanting to witness it first hand.

Disbelieving that Austin hammered Jack so badly, the other riders jumped on their bikes and challenged him one at a time. Loathing his missed opportunity to beat Austin at anything, Ben watched grounded on the sidelines as one-by-one Austin outrode them all. Getting more upset with each win, Ben glanced at Austin's bike with malicious intent. Another rider interrupted his destructive thoughts.

"Can I ride your bike next?" the rider asked.

"It's not the bike, you moron!" Ben snapped back sarcastically.

Clearly, Austin had a gift.

---

With the day drawing to a close, the warm afternoon weather felt more like summer than spring. All the other riders had already loaded up their bikes and taken off. Austin's bike and Jack's bike were parked next to Gary's home shop, a state-of-the-art building that was used just for motorcycles.

The huge roll-up door was open. Inside,

Austin could see an entire wall lined with restored vintage dirtbikes. The old Maaco's, CZ's, Husquvarna's, Ossa's, and Bultaco's were impressive. Austin smiled when he saw a little 1980 Honda fifty. Perfectly restored, it was nearly twenty-five years old and the same year as his very first dirtbike. The tank even had a small dent in the same exact place.

In the wash bay outside the shop, Jack pressure-washed the dirt from his bike as Austin wiped down his wet bike with a clean chamois.

"What kind of bars you want?" Jack asked Austin.

"Pro Tapers. With grips," Austin replied.

Austin looked up when a new yellow Volkswagen Bug pulled into Jack's driveway. The driver, an attractive girl about their age, pulled up next to the shop and turned the car off. She waited in the car as Amanda, Jack's girlfriend, got out and strutted up to them.

Jack flipped the pressure washer switch off and grinned at her. The way she dressed triggered something in him. Amanda's low-cut Fox t-shirt showed her voluptuous figure and her skin-tight jeans left little to anyone's imagination.

"Hey Jack," Amanda whined, "you wanna go for a *ride*?" She knew exactly what she wanted and how to get it. Flirting like a broke hooker, she stood with her hips off to one side and folded her arms across her chest. Squeezing her breasts together with her arms to show off her cleavage, she was every mother's worst nightmare. And every teenage boy's dream.

"Already did," grinned Jack, apparently missing her cue. "Just finished kicking Austin's ass."

Austin shook his head at Jack's nonsense and looked up at Amanda. Amanda dropped her arms and mustered a pathetic hello.

Austin nodded. He knew she didn't like him. He didn't have enough to offer, he suspected. Austin was good at reading people and knew that getting involved with girls like her only led to trouble.

But, what the heck. Austin stole a quick glance at her chest as he threw his leg over his bike and kicked it to a start. No harm in looking.

His bike had performed pretty well for an old machine that had been ridden all day long, but all of a sudden it was running unusually rough.

"A fine piece of equipment you got there," Jack said, sarcastically pointing out the obvious.

"Might need jets too," Austin ignored his teasing. "Sure you won't get nailed for it?"

"I do the inventory," Jack said. "He won't even know they're gone," Jack paused, grinned at Amanda then added, "unless I run out of vodka."

"Yeah, sure. Whatever you need," Austin said as he clicked his bike into gear. "See you later."

When Austin rode past the car, the driver

smiled at him. Caught off guard by her bright, blue sparkling eyes and her shiny, shoulder-length hair, Austin did a double-take and turned around to look at her again.

Already past the car, he could only see her eyes as she watched him in the rear view mirror. She smiled and coyly looked away, but then watched him again until he was out of sight. After Austin disappeared over the crest of the road, the girl turned her attention back to Amanda and Jack.

Amanda threw her arms over Jack's shoulders and leaned into him. She trailed her tongue up the side of his neck to his ear.

"Thought you didn't hang with losers," she said.

"Everyone I ride against is a loser," Jack grinned. He was pretty sure of himself.

Amanda hopped up on Jack, wrapped her legs around his waist and kissed him. Jack quickly switched gears from bikes to babes.

"Besides," Jack added, "he promised to get me a bottle for Friday night. Now, about that *ride*."

"Brooke's waiting in the car. Thought Ben might like to meet her," Amanda said.

"Ben split. Come on. It won't take long," Jack said.   Grinning, Jack lowered Amanda to the ground and hollered at Brooke as he pulled Amanda into the shop.

"Be right back!"

## Chapter 4 – MOTIVATION

In the middle of a shabby industrial park was a run down two-story concrete building. Big roll-up shop doors opened onto a cracked blacktop driveway. Offices with dirty windows looked out over the parking lot and metals yard.

The once-white painted concrete block interior walls were now almost completely covered with black welding soot. It was cramped, dark and dirty.

When a whistle blew, welders dressed in burned and tattered coveralls turned off their torches and flipped up their hoods. Lit cigarettes dangled from the lips of old, wrinkled faces that were also covered with black soot and grime.

Steve took off his welder's hood and ran a dirty hand through his greasy hair. He tapped a welder, who was still working, on the shoulder.

"Hey! Time's up!"

The welder turned off his torch and lifted his hood. It was Austin. He hung his hood on his welding tanks and headed for Steve's truck. He couldn't get out of there fast enough.

An old welder hollered after him, "You did good your first week, kid. Stick around and have a drink."

"No thanks," Austin yelled back as he got into the truck and slammed the door shut.

Steve walked casually up to the truck,

opened the driver's door and pulled a bottle of vodka from behind the seat. He filled up his coffee cup and walked back to the group without saying a word to Austin.

Forty-five minutes later and finally on their way home, Steve looked over at Austin slumped in his seat.

"What's your problem?"

"I don't know how you can work there," Austin said. "I can't breathe in that place."

"It's a good place to work. Management stays in the office and leaves us alone. You'll get used to it. I did," Steve shrugged. "Besides, if you want money for bike parts you gotta do the time."

Steve liked his job. He'd been there nearly twenty years. He knew Austin would eventually appreciate having a steady paycheck. Money was a powerful motivator.

Austin stared out the truck window. The dead weeds blurred into gray sidewalks as they sped along. To him, it felt like a prison sentence. Torture. Underneath it all, he was afraid that if he worked there too long, he would become one of them. Become his dad. But he desperately needed money for his bike and the upcoming racing season. At this point he knew he didn't have a better option.

Steve pulled the truck into a parking space at the strip mall. Austin watched him as he got out of the pickup and went into the pawnshop.

At the counter, Steve took off his gold

watch and put forty bucks into his front pocket as Nick, the owner, tagged the watch.

Nick and Steve had known each other since high school, and Steve had done business with him occasionally over the years – usually around Christmas. Recently, however, his transactions had become more regular. Like clockwork, he pawned the same watch for the same amount every two weeks.

"Thanks, Nick," Steve said. "Catch ya later."

"See you in two weeks," Nick said.

Disgusted, Austin watched as Steve walked out of the pawnshop without his watch and into the liquor store next door.

## Chapter 5 – OPPORTUNITY

The yellow flashing lights on the bus switched to red as the bus came to a stop in front of Coast Range Cycle. The business was clean, up-scale and flashy. The white building was freshly painted and the signs were clean and brightly lit. The parking lot and curbs were well maintained. The rows of gleaming motorcycles lined up out front always drew stares from people driving by. Austin understood the important link between projecting a good public image and success.

Hoping to get the parts for his bike that Jack promised, Austin hopped off the bus and looked around the parking lot for Jack's truck. He didn't find it so he headed for the building. When he walked past the rows of brand new bikes that lined the front of the building, he stopped and looked at them. Someday...

The place was busy for a Monday. Cindy counted change to a customer at the retail register at a quick pace. Three more people waited at the parts counter. The sales manager was doing the paperwork for a man and his young son who was perched on a new KX80.

"Hi, Cindy," Austin said. "Is Jack around?

"He hasn't shown up from school yet."

"Mind if I wait?" Austin asked.

"Sure," she smiled. "No problem."

Austin headed straight for the showroom and looked over the rows of sparkling motorcycles. Carefully, he scrutinized the new 2004 KTM's. He squatted down and looked at the engines at eye level. On the outside, they looked almost identical to the 2003's. But he knew from reading the trade magazines that they were quite a bit different than last year's model.

Thinking Jack had arrived, Austin looked up when a man entered the showroom and signaled Cindy for help. He watched Cindy give the man a quick nod as she waited on the next person in line.

"This place is busy. Where the heck is Jack?" Austin wondered.

Pulled back into his daydream, his fantasy, Austin ran his hand along the smooth seat of a SX250. Someday he'd have one.

"Can I get some help over here?" The customer's raised voice floated across the showroom just as the phone rang.

Austin looked up from the bike and saw Cindy nod at him again, then answer the phone. Seeing this, the man impatiently headed for the door. Austin glanced at Cindy then rushed over to the customer.

"Sorry for the delay," Austin apologized. "Did you have a question?"

"Wondering about the SX250's," the man said sharply. "I heard KTM made some changes this year."

The customer walked over to the same bike Austin was looking at just a few moments before. It was just like Ben's bike - the one Austin rode at Jack's practice track.

"They changed the exhaust ports but reworked the heads to increase compression," Austin explained pointing toward the parts he was talking about. "But, just like last year's model, it still has massive low-end thrust and a smooth climb onto the meat of the powerband that doesn't get out of control."

Austin didn't miss a beat. It was obvious he knew what he was talking about, which put the customer at ease.

"It's dependable, predictable and..." Austin grinned in proud remembrance, "wicked fast."

Cindy looked up and saw Austin pointing out different features to the customer.

"Would you buy one?" the customer asked Austin.

"In a heartbeat!" Austin replied.

The customer, pondering his decision, looked Austin straight in the eyes for a few, cool seconds.

"Okay then. I'll take it. What's your name?"

Austin stuck out his hand and looked back at the man. He knew the importance of eye contact as they shook. It conveyed honesty, integrity and respect.

"Austin. Good decision," Austin grinned. "He can do the paperwork for you right over there." Austin pointed to the sales manager, who was just finishing up with the KX80.

"Just curious?" the customer asked. "What's your commission on a bike like this? Five, ten percent?"

"Don't know exactly," Austin stammered. He hated being caught off guard. "Depends on the bike, I guess."

Austin stopped and looked at the bike. The calculator in his head was running at record speed. After the customer walked over to the sales desk, Austin walked quickly over to Cindy, who was still working with customers at the service counter.

"Is Gary here?" he urgently interrupted.

"He's in the shop," she said, with a slight look of concern. "But go on back."

Gary was helping a technician with a bike when Austin walked into the shop. He looked up briefly, then continued working. Behind schedule and annoyed at Jack's tardiness, Gary's tone was gruff and all business.

"Jack's not here," he stated.

"I was wondering if I could talk to you a minute."

"Make it quick," Gary said. "We're backed up."

"I'd like to apply for that sales job," Austin stated.

Gary glanced sideways at the technician in annoyed disbelief. He liked Austin, but didn't have time for this. Austin shuffled nervously.

"You have to know each bike we sell inside and out," Gary said. "And be able to read people. Know what they want."

Austin sensed his lack of interest and sold himself like the desperate hard-core salesman he could be.

"Look," Austin pressed, "I'm dependable and hardworking. I'll be here seven days a week if you need it. And I'll work for straight commission. If I don't meet your quota, you won't owe me a thing. C'mon. What do you say?"

"You have any references?" Gary asked as he looked back at the bike he was working on. He already knew the answer to the question. This conversation was over.

"Yeah," Austin replied. "The guy in the showroom. I just sold him a KTM SX250."

## Chapter 6 – DEPENDABILITY

With the start of the racing season just around the corner, everyone was getting their bike into shape and spending more time in the seat. Except Austin.

Now into his third week at the bike shop, Austin struggled to balance work and school. He worked every day after school and ten hours on Saturday. Weekdays, he rode home at six o'clock, ate dinner, then tackled his homework. Because he knew that getting a scholarship was the only chance he had of going to college, Austin took the hardest advanced classes that were offered and worked hard to make straight A's. Five hours a night at the kitchen table was about average.

His dad didn't say a word when Austin quit his welding job. No encouragement, no argument. Nothing. Austin thought it was strange how Steve just ignored the whole thing.

Not wanting to push the envelope, Austin never asked his dad for a ride to work. Instead, he rode his dirtbike, which wasn't street legal,on the backroads to and from the shop. Because he knew getting caught would be expensive, he kept a close look-out for cop cars.

It was another busy afternoon at Coast Range Cycle and the phone never stopped ringing. Austin was with a customer on the sales floor when the man and his young son rolled the new KX80, now crashed, toward Cindy at the retail counter. She answered the ringing phone just as the man walked up to her and made eye contact.

"Coast Range Cycle."

"Service?" he asked her.

Cindy held the phone in one hand and pointed toward a line of customers at the service counter. Only two service techs were at the computers. *Where the heck is Jack?* she thought to herself. Annoyed, she scanned the room and waved at Austin. Austin nodded at her.

"Take a look at this comparison while you're thinking about it," Austin told his customer. "I'll be right back."

At the service counter, Austin clicked away on the keyboard at the third computer terminal.

"What can I do for you?" he asked the man and grinned at the boy.

"Fix it," the man said.

"Don't you want an estimate first?" Austin asked.

"No. Just fix it. We have a race this weekend."

Austin nodded. Now he understood. He grinned at the boy and raised his eyebrows.

"Washougal?" Austin asked.

"Yup," the boy, full of pride, nodded.

Austin looked back and forth from the bike to the screen and typed as he spoke.

"Okay. It's a 2003 KX80. Let's start with the front end. New rim. Front fork. Brake lever. Bars are bent too."

The man took a deep breath and motioned for Austin to keep going.

"What'd ya hit?" Austin asked the boy.

"My mom's new car," he sheepishly confessed.

"Ouch," Austin winced. "Need a new helmet, I bet."

"Better throw one in," the man said.

"How about some new gloves too?" Austin suggested.

"You work on commission?" the man asked.

A little embarrassed, Austin shrugged and smiled. He didn't want it to be quite that obvious. The man threw a credit card on the counter. Austin laid an invoice in front of him to sign.

"Okay, your total's six hundred twenty-three dollars. Sign and we'll have it ready Friday evening," Austin stated, then grinned at the boy again. "Just in time for the race."

Austin wished the boy good luck and hurried back to his customer in the showroom, who was still undecided.

---

A short time later, Gary came out of the office and walked over to the service counter.

"Heard from Jack yet?" he asked Cindy.

"Not yet," she said as she looked at the clock.

Gary noticed the KX80 sitting in front of the service desk and walked over to it. "Who left this here?" he asked the service techs. Still with customers, they nodded toward Austin.

Gary grabbed hold of the handlebars, wheeled the motorcycle into the shop and parked it next to fifteen other bikes that waited to be serviced or repaired. He pulled the invoice out of the plastic and reviewed it. He was both surprised and impressed at the total.

"Damn. Good job." Gary said out loud.

One of the technicians looked up from the bike he was working on. As soon as Gary left the shop, he walked over and looked at the invoice. "The kid just might make it," he said to the other technician.

---

When things slowed down, Gary and Cindy pulled Austin aside and reviewed KTM sales trends on the office computer. Gary explained what Coast Cycle's market share was compared to other dealerships, where they wanted to be by the end of the year and how sales in the coming summer racing season would affect the overall goal.

When the front doors opened, Cindy, Gary and Austin looked up. They watched Jack and

Ben strolled lazily through the showroom and shuffled toward the service counter. To Austin, it was obvious they were stoned. He looked quickly at Gary and Cindy but they didn't seem to notice. Or maybe they didn't want to notice.

Jack wore baggy jeans, a white t-shirt, Vans, and thick hoop earrings in both ears. Even though Austin knew Jack's clothes were expensive, he thought they looked terrible. Ben was dressed the same except in place of the t-shirt, he wore a white wifebeater tank to draw attention to his tatts.

"Where the heck have you been?" Cindy demanded. "We've been swamped."

"Detention. I cut a class after lunch," Jack mumbled.

"Yeah, he lost track of time eating..." Ben said. Under his breath he added, "Amanda."

Cindy's mouth dropped open.

"Shut the heck up!" Gary snapped. "You're not a real fast learner are you, Ben?"

"You know the rules, Jack," Cindy sternly reminded him. "C's or better or you don't ride. You have to go to class to make the grades. Motocrossers have a short career. You gotta have a back-up plan."

"How long is your detention this time?" Gary asked.

"Just a week. It's no big deal," Jack said.

"It will be if I don't let you race, won't it?" Gary quipped. "And take that crap out of your ears when you're in here. This is a business, not a freak show."

Gary worked hard to grow his business. He and Cindy started Coast Range Cycle fifteen years ago when Jack was just a toddler. They had a small building and even smaller sales revenue. Now he was the second largest dealer in the state and well respected in the motorcycle community. He hoped Jack would take over the business some day. But given Jack's choices, Gary wondered how realistic that dream was.

Jack put his earrings in his pockets and went to work at the service counter. The other service techs looked at each other but said nothing.

Jack knew how they felt about him, but he didn't care. He was the typical owner's kid. He didn't appreciate that silver spoon in his mouth. To him, it felt like a gag.

After he finished studying the sales trends, Austin walked over to Jack.

"Hey, dude. You okay?" Austin asked.

"Yeah, sure," Jack answered.

Gary walked up behind them and handed Jack a race entry form.

"Here," Gary said to Jack. "Fill this out."

"You gonna race this weekend?" Jack asked Austin.

From across the room Austin saw a young woman walk into the retail section and flip through the racks of motocross gear.

"I don't know. Maybe," Austin said, distracted by the young woman. She looked familiar.

Austin walked over to the retail section. Gary hollered after him, "Clear it with your dad first, okay?"

Austin looked back, nodded, then walked up beside the young woman who was quickly flipping through the hangers on the rack. Austin, back to being the salesman, tried to be professional, but couldn't quite hide his piqued interest and pounding pulse.

"Hi," Austin said. "Can I help you find something?"

"Yeah," the young woman said without looking up. "I need a pair of motocross pants. Size five."

Austin suddenly noticed the small boy holding her hand. He squatted down to his level.

"Hey buddy. What color?"

"Blue and white. Like my bike," the little boy answered.

Austin stood up and pulled a pair of motocross pants from the rack.

"Thor's a good brand. Try these on, Yamaha man."

After Austin pointed the little boy in the direction of the dressing room, the young woman turned to him and smiled. He smiled back and noticed that his heart was suddenly pounding.

"You're good with kids," she said. "Have we met?"

Trying to hide his nervousness, Austin

went to the rack and picked out a small pair of matching gloves.

"Aren't you the new girl? Amanda's friend?" Austin asked.

"Yeah, right," she said. "Hi. I'm Brooke. And that's Bobby." Brooke pointed toward the dressing room.

"Austin," he said and stuck out his hand. Brooke giggled and shook his hand. Austin felt foolish for instinctively shaking her hand and wondered why moments like this always had to be so awkward.

"Do you race?" Brooke asked.

Austin stammered, "Umm..."

"Of course you do," Brooke said, slightly embarrassed, "You work here."

Outfitted in the new pants, Bobby strutted up to them and broke the awkward tension. Austin handed him a pair of gloves. Back to business.

"The pants fit good. How about some new gloves?" he asked.

"Sure!" Bobby exclaimed.

"Thanks for your help," Brooke said as she smiled at Austin.

"No problem," he smiled back. "Hey, maybe I'll see you at the race."

"Sure," Brooke replied, still smiling.

A short time later, it was closing time and quickly getting dark. Jack, always the first one to leave, left right at six. Austin waited with Cindy and Gary while they closed down and locked the back door from the outside.

"Great job today, Austin," Cindy said. "You're a natural at sales."

"Thanks," Austin replied. "It's easy. I like people."

"See you tomorrow," Gary said.

"Night." Austin said as he walked over to his bike. He put on his helmet, started his bike and took off through the alley. No lights, no tags.

Just ahead on the main road, Austin saw a police car and quickly turned his bike onto a side street. He looked back. The cop car turned and followed him. Austin turned into an alley and gassed it. A sharp right, then left, and he was out of the city limits.

When he looked back, it was all clear. Leaving a cloud of dust behind him, Austin screamed his bike up the long dirt road. Seven miles later, he let off the throttle and coasted quietly into his driveway.

Back at Coast Range Cycle, the officer got out of his patrol car and tried the front door. It was locked. He'd have to come back tomorrow.

Steve was just getting home and walked toward the house carrying his lunch box and another bottle of booze in a brown paper bag. Austin coasted up to him, killed his bike and tried to build his nerve.

"I'm gonna race with Jack tomorrow," Austin said keeping his distance. "Gary's treat for doin' a good job at the shop."

Steve stopped mid-movement, glared at Austin, then stormed into the house and slammed the door.

Austin dropped his head. Oh well, it was worth it.

The next day at the crack of dawn, Austin paced near Gary's home shop door deep in thought. The spring air was crisp and cool and felt good on his hot face. He ran his tongue over his freshly bruised lip. His guilt faded in and out as his thoughts switched gears and bounced back and forth from his love of racing to his dad's violent outbursts. Austin didn't notice Gary and Jack walk from the house to the shop.

"Dang! You actually showed up," Jack mocked.

Austin jerked back to reality. Too late now. Screw the old man. "You know it," Austin said.

Gary helped Austin load his bike into the trailer and supervised Austin while he tugged on the tie downs.

"Where's your gear?" Gary asked Austin.

"Outgrew everything. Waiting for my first paycheck."

"Jack, go round up some of the old gear," Gary said. "What size are your feet, Austin?"

"Eleven," Austin said.

"Your old boots should fit him," Gary said to Jack. "And hurry up. We still gotta pick up Ben."

As Gary started his diesel crew cab pickup, Jack came back in a huff with boots, goggles, a chest protector, faded pants, jersey, and worn out gloves - all wadded up in a ball.

Jack shoved them at Austin and said, "*Looking* like you can win is half your edge."

Holding Jack's old gear, Austin climbed into the back seat of the fancy pickup. He knew Jack was getting tired of having him around all the time, but he wasn't about to turn down Gary's offer. After they picked up Ben, they headed north to Washougal, Washington for the first race of the season.

---

Later that same morning, Steve stood in the front doorway of his house. Unshaven and scruffy, he watched the police officer walk back to the patrol car.

"Thanks for coming by, Officer," Steve hollered after him. "I'll take care of it."

## Chapter 7 – HUMILITY

Covering over three hundred acres, the Washougal Motocross Track was a labyrinth of dirt that wound through a forest of fir trees and open fields. In contrast to the bright green grass, the brown dirt of the tight hairpins, huge tabletops, whoops, rhythm sections, and jumps added a harsh-cut edge to an otherwise picture-perfect landscape.

The expansive pit section already buzzed with pre-race activity. The parking lot was packed with pickup trucks, motorcycle trailers, motorhomes, and hundreds of motocross bikes and their riders. The excitement was thick and contagious. Especially for Austin.

Gary found a place to park and unlocked the trailer. Austin dropped Jack's old gear into a pile and helped wheel out the bikes. With room in the trailer to move around, the four racers went inside to get dressed.

Gary, Jack and Ben emerged from the trailer confident and proud. Dressed in full motocross gear, they carried their helmets like soldiers ready for battle. Ben wore the latest black, blue and orange Fox gear. Gary, racing his TM in the over-forty class, donned the standard blue and yellow TM Racing apparel. Jack wore brand new reflective silver gear from Fleshgear and large silver hoop earrings in both ears. Reflecting the sun's rays, he looked like a star in more ways than one.

Still in the trailer, Austin dug through the pile of old motocross gear and got dressed. After he snapped on the chest protector, he looked down at himself, shook his head and took a deep breath. He wondered if Jack was playing a good-natured joke on him or was being cruel.

Austin stepped out of the trailer looking like a confused Power Ranger. He had on Kawasaki green motocross pants, a faded orange jersey with a huge hole in one of the elbows, one yellow glove, one blue glove, and worn-out white boots. Of course nothing matched the chest protector or his old helmet.

Ben saw him first and laughed so hard he started to cough, then choke. When Gary turned to see what all the commotion was about, his jaw dropped. He shook his head in disbelief and glared at Jack.

Jack turned his back on the group to hide his smile and walked over to his Honda.

The bikes, lined up like cavalry horses begging to be raced, were spotlessly clean and fully fueled. Their black three digit numbers stood out against white plates. A "001" on Jack's numberplate, a "333" on Ben's, and a "287" on Austin's.

"C'mon," Gary said, "We have time before the start. Let's go watch the little guys."

At the miniature motocross track for the

little kids, Gary, Jack, Ben, and Austin mixed into the crowd and stood at the edge of a small oval of freshly groomed dirt. The track was complete with little whoops, a small jump, and a short back straight.

On the chalked starting line, ten riders twisted throttles and revved their tiny 50cc engines. Each kid wore miniature motocross gear and tried to act like the pros. They put on the meanest race-face a five-year-old could possibly muster.

Dads paced behind their sons. Moms bounced and shouted encouragingly from the sidelines.

Brooke clapped and yelled, "Come on, Bobby. You can do it!" Bobby quickly gave Brooke a blue and white gloved thumbs-up. Along with a huge smile, she gave him one back.

Ron Heben, a KTM scout dressed in an orange polo shirt and black slacks, grinned as he watched the race. His organizer, palm pilot, and stopwatch were momentarily forgotten. Overflowing with natural charisma and charm, everyone liked and respected him. They also knew how important he was.

The flag dropped and the little riders raced around the track. At the first turn, two bikes crashed and dads ran to the rescue. Bobby and the other riders kept racing.

Bill Mitchell, a Fox rep, walked up to Ron and stuck his hand out.

"Hi Ron. Good to see you," he said. Ron shook his hand.

"Hey Bill. Last year, Loretta's right?"

"Right. How's KTM treating you?" Bill asked.

Ron grinned, "Having a blast. Still with Fox?"

"Yep," Bill nodded. "What kind of talent are you looking for this year?"

"Good ones, but not this young," Ron joked as he watched the little riders roll carefully over the whoops. "Cute, aren't they?"

"Takes me back every time," Bill smiled.

"We'd like to add two riders in the two-fifty class and one in the one twenty-five class," Ron said, getting back to business. "We usually don't pick anyone up until after the Loretta Lynn Nationals, but heard there was some talent up here worth a look."

Bill pointed to Jack standing next to Gary, Austin and Ben. Jack stretched the neckline of his new silver jersey to scratch his shoulder. His tatts, now visible, crawled around his lower neck like centipedes.

"That's Jack Preston," Bill said. "He was the number one plate in the Northwest Region last year. Calls himself the Jack Attack."

Two fans in front of Ron and Bill overheard their conversation and snickered to each other, "Jack Ass is more like it."

Ron heard them, but didn't respond. Everyone seemed to have an opinion about what makes a good motocross racer. But, most people didn't understand the business side of racing.

Back at the little track, the young riders hit the small tabletop and got a few inches of air. The crowd clapped and cheered them on. Brooke was totally engrossed in the race and didn't notice Jack walk up beside her.

Even though he couldn't hear their conversation, Austin wondered about Jack's motives and watched them from the other side of the track.

"Hey, baby. Have we met?" Jack flirted.

Brooke pulled back in disbelief. "You're hitting on me?"

"Sure. Why not?" Jack said in a smart-aleck tone. He wasn't used to being rejected.

"Because I'm Amanda's friend," Brooke stated. "Remember?"

"Yeah, but she's not here," Jack said, giving it one more shot.

Brooke ignored him and went back to watching the race. She couldn't help but notice Ron and Bill standing across from her. Everyone noticed them. She wished she could hear their conversation and wondered if they were talking about the little racers. About Bobby.

"Along with good grades," Ron continued, "we emphasize appearance. Clean cut. No visible tatts. Clear, well-spoken English and no foul language."

"Hard to find now days," Bill stated.

"Sometimes. But these kids are at the top of their game and are expected to act like it," Ron said then added with a grin, "Along with having fun, of course."

"What about riding skills?" Bill asked.

"Maneuvering, cornering speed, line selection, technique and good decision-making on the track. Desire and dedication play the biggest part. It's not always about the win. But," Ron had to admit, "winning riders do sell bikes."

"And riding gear," Bill agreed. They focused their attention back on the end of the race as Bobby rode past the waving checkered flag. Jumping like a cheerleader, Brooke yelled and clapped. Jack grinned as he watched her chest bounce.

A few minutes later, Bobby ran over to Brooke with his new trophy. Brooke squatted down and gave him a big hug. Jack quickly stepped back. Brooke watched him walk away and smiled.

"Works every time," she said as she caught sight of Austin standing next to Ben and Gary. Holding Bobby's hand, Brooke walked up behind Austin.

"Hey, Austin. How's it going?" she asked.

Austin turned around and smiled at Brooke. He was proud that he one-upped Jack and had Brooke's attention, but he was still a little embarrassed about his gear.

"Hey. Good to see you," he said to Brooke.

He squatted down to Bobby's level and high-fived him. "Great job, buddy. Congratulations!"

"Thanks," Bobby smiled. "Yep, I did good!"

"What time do you race?" Brooke asked, "We'd like to watch."

"We're up after the pros," Austin replied.

"Cool," Brooke said.

"I should be pretty easy to spot." Austin looked down at his rainbow gear and laughed.

"Yeah," she teased him. "You look... interesting."

Brooke liked Austin's confidence and his ability to laugh at himself. But, she'd also heard rumors about Austin's dad and what kind of life Austin had. It was obvious that his family didn't have money. He didn't have a car and she had seen his run-down house, which Amanda was quick to point out. But, Brooke also knew he was the senior class Valedictorian and he never complained about anything.

"Hey, we're all getting together Friday night at Paradise Pizza next to Coast Range Cycle. Would you like to join us?" Brooke asked then quickly added, "I can give you a ride."

Austin's heart started to pound again. He wanted a shot with her, but figured if she knew he lived in a dilapidated house out in the sticks with an alcoholic father, his chances would evaporate.

"My house is...," Austin paused, "too far

out of town."

"Amanda showed me where you live. It's not that far," Brooke replied.

Because Austin knew how Amanda operated, he wasn't surprised that Brooke already knew where he lived. He was surprised that it didn't matter to Brooke.

Austin saw Jack whisper something to Ben. Both of them turned and watched him. Austin wasn't going to back down now.

"Cool. Okay. Sure," Austin said.

Just then, a thirty-something man pushed Bobby's bike up behind Brooke. When Brooke saw the man, she instantly stopped flirting and stepped away from Austin.

"Let's go," the man said sternly.

"See you later," Brooke said.

Bobby let go of Brooke's hand and took his bike by the handlebars. As they walked away, the man draped his arm over Brooke's shoulders.

Jack and Ben stepped up to Austin. Even they were surprised. Gary walked over and caught the tail end of their conversation.

"She's married?" Austin gasped.

"Sick. That ought to be illegal," Jack said.

"Sucks to be her," Ben said, "but I could be him."

Gary rolled his eyes at Ben's classless remarks. "We're up. Let's go."

---

Seventy-five riders lined up at the starting gate according to class and revved their engines. The bikes produced an exhilarating roar and filled the air with sweet smelling fumes.

Twenty-five pros in the first wave positioned their bikes against the drop bar and mentally selected their line. Like crouched panthers, they were ready to spring.

Like a funnel, the track narrowed from fifty feet to twenty feet in less than twenty-five yards, then suddenly banked left. From years of experience, each rider knew the importance of making the holeshot.

Right behind the pros, twenty-two other riders in the 250 class flanked Austin, Jack, and Ben. Austin looked down the line at Jack, who was several riders away. When Jack flipped him off, Austin flipped him back with a nod. Ben leaned forward on his bike and gave Austin an agressive arm signal - an overstated version of the finger. Austin didn't bother to respond.

Suddenly, the gate dropped. The twenty-five pro riders blasted toward the first corner and funneled through it with beautiful perfection. Their race was on! Waiting in the next wave, Austin wished he could watch it, but only for a second. Doing it was, without question, way more fun.

A pit man signaled Austin's wave. The riders pulled up to the gates and waited with jaw-clenching anticipation for the start. Austin closed his eyes for a second.

"My choice. My way." Austin opened his eyes just as the gate dropped.

Engines screamed as bikes bolted off the line in unison, and went into the corner only inches apart. Making the holeshot, Jack came out of the corner in the lead. Austin twisted his throttle and blasted out of the corner in third place right behind Ben. Both of them barely escaped the five-rider pile-up behind them. Seven more riders carefully wove through the wreck then sped ahead.

Looking like a high-tech carnival ride, riders and colors blurred past the crowd. Engines screamed. Mud flew. Fans cheered. Bikes went down. It was fast-paced motocross racing at its dangerous best.

From their vantage point in the tower, Ron and Bill could see most of the track and followed the riders they were interested in. At the end of each lap, Ron looked at his stopwatch and recorded the times on his palm pilot. Impressed, he showed the times to Bill.

On the last lap, Ben did a double-take when Austin passed him on the inside of a tight corner. Surprised because he thought Austin was weak in the corners, Ben twisted the throttle with renewed vengeance and followed Austin dangerously close. He wasn't about to let Austin beat him.

Inside his mud sprayed goggles, Austin's eyes shifted from side to side as he tried to see behind him without turning his head. He didn't trust Ben and wanted to put as much distance between them as possible.

Screaming his bike all out, Ben passed Austin on the rhythm section and quickly looked back at him. Austin saw the flat straightaway ahead, gassed it and kept the pressure on. He knew he could pass Ben on that stretch of the track.

So did Ben. To make sure that didn't happen, he pulled in the clutch and braced himself. When the moment was right, Ben stomped his foot down on the back brake.

Not expecting the sudden slowdown, Austin slammed into Ben's back tire, lost control and was pitched over the handlebars.

Ben felt the impact, but never looked back.

As Ben sped away, Austin frantically tried to keep the bike from going down and fought to regain control. But in seconds, Austin lost the battle and went down with his bike.

In a clumsy and awkward wreck, his left hand was skewered into the dirt by the end of the handlebar. As the small bones in his hand snapped, pain shot through his fingers and burned inside his palm like fuel exploding in the cylinder.

Another rider flew by Austin. In a frantic hurry, Austin ignored the searing hot pain in his left hand, picked the bike up and took off again. Like he was trying to catch the devil himself, he passed rider after rider in a blur as he looked for

Ben. But the race was over. Austin flew by the checkered flags with only a few riders in his class behind him.

And Ron witnessed the whole thing.

At the end of the day, Ron and Bill visited while they waited for the crowd to clear out. Getting into the track was easy. Some people showed up the night before and camped, but most people arrived in gradual waves over the course of the morning. However when the races were over, everyone wanted to leave at once. Because there was only one two-lane country road leading to Highway 14, getting out of Washougal took hours.

Ron watched Austin, dressed in his rainbow gear, make his way back to the pits. He saw Austin high-five the KX80 boy who was standing next to his newly repaired motorcycle and a large trophy.

Nursing his left hand, Austin kept it gloved and close to his body as he talked to the boy and admired his trophy. When Gary walked by and motioned toward the trailer, Austin shook the kid's hand.

"It ran really good," the kid exclaimed.

"I'd have to give all the credit to the rider," Austin smiled. "I gotta go. Congratulations!"

Austin rode his bike up to the trailer. He couldn't help but notice the two trophies that sat on the floor next to the open door. Gary had taken second place in his class; Jack took first in his.

With Gary's bike already loaded, Jack, Ben, and Austin took turns loading their dirty bikes and securing the tie-downs. Even though it was throbbing in pain, Austin kept his wounded hand gloved and his injury concealed.

"Like riding my butt, Austin?" Ben smirked as they finished.

Jack latched and locked the trailer door. Austin was in too much pain to respond and ignored Ben.

"You know that kind of crap will get you eighty-six'd from the track," Jack said to Ben.

"Screw you, Jack," Ben snapped. "I didn't do nothin' you haven't done."

## Chapter 8 – COMPASSION

Austin got off the school bus and looked around the school parking lot. Holding his left hand inside his jacket, he walked over to Jack, who threw his driving glasses on the dash and got out of his pickup.

"Hey," Austin said to Jack. "I got a problem. I think it's broke." Austin held out his left hand. It was swollen twice the normal size. A black and blue handlebar ring was imprinted on his palm.

"Bet that hurts, but I ain't your frickin' mother," Jack said.

"Come on Jack," Austin said. "We don't have insurance. What should I do?"

Jack thought for a second then grabbed his glasses off the dash.

"Shit. Get in. Give me your wallet," Jack demanded.

Ten minutes later, Jack pulled his truck into the hospital parking lot and walked with Austin to the emergency room. Just inside the door, Austin sat down and gingerly laid his bruised and swollen left hand on the triage nurse's desk. The nurse turned to her computer.

"Ouch. Let's get you looked at. Name?"

"Jack Preston," Austin said. Austin removed Jack's license and insurance card from his own wallet and slid it across the desk.

"Here's my license and insurance card. All the info is right there," Austin lied.

The nurse quickly glanced from the ID picture of Jack wearing glasses to Austin, who was wearing Jack's glasses. Close enough. She turned to her keyboard and entered his information.

---

Later that night, Austin fumbled tools as he tried to work on his carburetor at his workbench in the basement shop. His left hand was in a bright white cast that extended from his black and blue knuckles to six inches above his wrist.

Steve, who was intoxicated again, paced nervously back and forth as their conversation quickly turned into an explosive argument.

"Why should I quit? I told you, worker's comp covered it!" Austin protested and raised his broken hand in the air. "It's not going to cost you a thing!"

"Because the cops were here! You know your bike isn't street legal. I can't afford a ticket," Steve fired back.

"I can outrun anybody in eight miles, including the cops. I need that job!" Austin yelled. "I won't quit!"

Steve walked toward him at a quick pace. Realizing he stepped over that line again, Austin stopped working.

"No!" Steve yelled back. "You're through! YOU HEAR ME? You will quit!"

"Why do you hold me down? When I turned seventeen, you *all-of-a-sudden* wanted me to quit racing. Now I can't even work at the shop?" The idea of having to quit his job pushed Austin over the edge. He didn't care anymore about that line. "What's the real reason, Dad!" Austin screamed. "Afraid I might make something out of my life?"

"You watch your damn mouth!" Steve demanded. Only six inches away from Austin's face now, spit flew as Steve yelled. He clenched his fist at his side, but Austin didn't back down.

Austin glared at him, leaned into his face and sneered, "Why don't you go have another drink?"

With the speed and crack of lightening, Steve backhanded Austin and sent him flying into his motorcycle. Once on the ground, Austin didn't move. He knew better than to get up. Shock, then anger, radiated from his eyes as blood trickled from the corner of his mouth.

"Next time you'd better keep your goddamn mouth shut!" Steve warned.

Austin watched Steve stagger out of the room. At this moment, he hated his dad. Really hated him.

For a long time, Austin sat motionless against his bike and stared at the wall. As he held a bloody rag against his lip, his eyes blinked away hot, angry tears. For the first time ever, he thought about how unfair his life seemed. Why couldn't he have a dad like Gary?

"Austin...you in here?" Brooke called, interrupting Austin's unusual bout of self-pity.

Austin quickly stood up and tried to pull himself together. He wiped at his eyes with the bloody rag then quickly squatted back down and pretended to work on his bike.

"Hey. I knocked on the front door, but nobody answered," Brooke said.

She wore jeans, which fit perfectly, and a cute pink t-shirt. Her outfit complimented her slender and well-proportioned body. She carried a soda from the fast food restaurant and took a sip from the straw. A clear coat of lip-gloss made her lips shine.

Austin missed her entrance and kept his back to Brooke. "Didn't hear you, that's all."

"Ready to go?" she asked.

On account of what he saw at the track, Austin had already written off their date.

Brooke walked around the bike and squatted in front of Austin. Cautiously he looked up at her over the bike's framework. Instantly startled, Brooke stood up.

"Oh my God! What happened?" she asked in shock.

Austin's lip was bruised dark purple. Blood still gushed from the corner of his mouth. His jaw was tender and swollen. Blood from the rag was smeared all over his face.

"It's not bad, really," Austin said.

"Who did this?" she demanded.

"It doesn't matter."

"It was Ben, wasn't it?" Brooke asked. "That jerk. I overheard him talking to Jack about it."

"No," Austin cut her off, "it was my dad. All right?"

Brooke was instantly silenced. She looked toward the door as if she was worried for her own safety.

"Go ahead and leave. I'll be fine. I always am," Austin said.

"No, it's okay. I'll stay." Brooke picked up a shop towel and wiped the blood from Austin's face. "Is your mom here?"

Austin gritted his teeth and refused to wince from the pain. "I was fourteen when she left. Dad use to lose it with her, too."

"Don't you miss her?"

"Yeah," Austin agreed. "But it was worse having her here. I was too little to stop him. At least this way she's safe."

"And now it's your turn." Brooke said, shaking her head.

"I can take it," Austin said.

"Why didn't you go with her?" she asked.

"She moved to San Diego, close to my grandma," Austin said. "Can't ride a dirtbike in the city. She calls sometimes."

Brooke never understood why people put up with abuse. She knew a girl once who finally stood up to an abusive boyfriend. After he realized she'd no longer play the victim, he left and found a new target – someone else he could control. That guy was never without someone to hit. Brooke wondered if abusers were secretly afraid of being alone.

Austin looked at her without saying anything and felt his heart start to pound again. She was really pretty. Her blue eyes still sparkled with confidence and energy. Her complexion was smooth and clear and her full lips were shaped perfectly for kissing. Beside the lip-gloss, the only makeup she wore was mascara. He didn't like a lot of makeup on women. She looked clean and fresh.

"How long have you been married?" he asked, trying to break the uncomfortable silence.

"I'm not married," Brooke laughed.

"Isn't Bobby...?" Austin was afraid to say it.

"My brother," Brooke answered for him.

"And the guy at the track?"

"My dad," she laughed. "I can't believe you thought I was married!"

Austin grinned. That was good news.

Brooke took the ice from her soda, wrapped it in a clean shop rag and handed it to Austin. He held it to his lip and sat down on the floor and leaned against the shop bench. Brooke sat down beside him.

"He looks so young," Austin commented.

"He got Mom pregnant with me when they were sixteen," Brooke confessed. "He gave up motocross to get a job and support us." Brooke took another drink from her soda then offered it to Austin. "That's why he pushes Bobby to race and is so overly protective of me. Doesn't want us to make the same mistakes."

Austin took a drink from her soda and looked at her quizzically, almost afraid to ask. Brooke sensed what he was thinking and filled in the gaps.

"My mom's gone too. I was twelve. She died during Bobby's delivery. I'm the only mom Bobby knows."

"That's rough," Austin said. "How do you cope?"

"My dad always says "W*e only get one life. Make it a good one.*" So, I choose to make it a good one. That's all."

Austin looked at her in awe. She was the first girl he'd met with that attitude. He agreed with it and instantly respected her.

"What do you want out of life, Austin? What's your dream?" Brooke asked.

Austin took a deep breath before he answered. "Just one shot at riding pro. Just one. I want to know if I'm good enough. I don't want to wake up someday and *wish I had*. Every day at work I see dads trying to buy their dreams back and live through their kids." He knew about people like Brooke's dad and hoped his words didn't offend her. "But not mine," he continued. "I don't know what he hates more – me or motorcycles."

## Chapter 9 – CHOICES

It was Saturday afternoon. After cashing his check at the bank, Steve went to the pawnshop. He handed Nick three twentys and put his watch back on.

"Thanks, Nick. See ya later."

That same day at Coast Range Cycle, Cindy handed out paychecks. Austin kissed the envelope.

"Thank you very much," he told Cindy.

Just before closing time, Austin picked out a new helmet and a new pair of goggles and laid them on the counter. Cindy cashed his check and rung up his gear.

"It comes to two hundred fifty-one," she said.

Austin looked at the price tags on the gear. "It should be more than that," he said.

"Don't forget about your employee discount," she smiled.

"Employee discount? Sweet! Thanks!" Austin was thrilled that he had money left over.

When Austin was finished with Cindy, Jack pulled him aside and asked, "Hey, how'd those bars work out?"

"Okay," Austin said.

"You need any more parts?" Jack asked.

"Man, I work here now," Austin said. "I can't steal from my boss. I'll buy what I need from now on."

Jack was miffed. "Well, that's mighty big of you but my bottle's empty and you still owe me!" Jack pointed to Austin's cast. Austin had hoped he was through dealing with Jack.

"Fine. Whatever," Austin conceded. "Stop by the house."

Austin turned away from Jack just as Steve stumbled through the front door of Coast Range Cycle. In an angry huff, Steve stormed straight toward Austin.

Realizing there was no way to escape the embarrassment, Austin braced himself for the impending scene. Just before Steve reached Austin, Gary walked out of the office and spotted him.

"Hey, Steve!" Gary hollered from across the room. "Great to see you! Man, it's been a while!"

Steve instantly switched gears. Gary walked over to him and shook his hand. Austin waited nervously next to Jack, suddenly not knowing what to expect.

"It has been a while," Steve agreed. "How've you been?"

"Doing great. Working too much," Gary said. "Do much riding?"

"No, working the overtime too. Hard to find decent welders any more. Seems like everyone went high-tech."

"They must be taking care of you," Gary said, noticing Steve's watch. "That's a fine watch."

Steve looked at his watch and quickly shrugged it off. "Thanks."

Steve glanced at a framed black and white photo that was hung on the wall. Three young riders on motorcycles posed for the picture. The only numberplate visible was number 179.

Gary saw Steve look at the picture and grinned.

"Remember that?" Gary asked. "Washougal's opening day the summer of 1972. You beat the heck out of me and took first place!"

Steve winced as he flashed back. For a second everything went white and his memory carried him back to 1972 and the Washougal track. The same familiar yellow haze. The 70's motocross rider speeding recklessly away from him toward the trees. Steve quickly closed his eyes as the rider in his mind hit the outside corner of the berm head on.

"Man you were fast!" Gary said, snapping Steve out of the vision. "You should have turned pro," he added. "Looks like Austin's got some of his old man in him. Last weekend he placed near the top ten."

"How's he workin' out down here?" Steve asked, eager to change the subject.

"Doing a great job. Glad he's aboard."

"Not many people would have kept him on after breaking his hand. Worker's comp and all. Thanks," Steve said.

Jack looked over at Austin and realized Austin had lied to Steve.

"If I fired all my employees that got hurt," Gary said apparently missing the details, "Cindy would be working alone. You know how it is - bikes or bodies. Something gets broke every race, including the wallet."

"Right," Steve agreed and shifted his focus back to Austin. "Well, it's good to see you. Let me know if he screws up, will ya?"

Steve headed for the door and glared at Austin as he passed him.

"See ya tonight, kid."

Austin dropped his head as Steve went out the door. "Here we go again," Austin said.

---

Later that evening at Austin's house, two new and unopened bottles of vodka sat on the kitchen counter. Austin looked at the bottles then glanced over his shoulder at the closed bathroom door. He heard Steve urinating.

With his hand still in a cast, Austin fumbled as he pulled an empty vodka bottle from the trash and filled it half full with vodka from the other bottle. Then he filled both bottles up with water and screwed the lids back on.

When he heard the toilet flush, Austin looked toward the bathroom door. In a rush, he grabbed a bottle, put it in the trashcan, then quietly closed the cabinet door. Two seconds later, Steve emerged from the bathroom. Trying to maintain his cool and not give anything away, Austin casually leaned against the counter in front of the cabinet that held the trashcan.

When Steve walked up to the counter to fix a drink, Austin noticed that both lids on the bottles had been opened. That meant the bottle in the trash was the straight stuff. Oh, well. No way to change it now. Austin grabbed a bottle off the counter and opened it for Steve, who looked at him but said nothing.

As Steve went through his usual routine of mixing a drink, Austin saw the muscles on his dad's jaw tighten and relax. He recognized the tension and knew that a confrontation was certain if he didn't get out of there. After Steve moved to the table, Austin opened the cabinet and quickly tied the trash bag shut.

Once outside, Austin removed the bottle and stashed it in the weeds next to the house. Ater he dropped the trash into the metal garbage can, he banged the lid in place as loud as he coud in hopes of erasing any suspicion his dad might have. Afterwards, Austin snatched up the bottle and went into the basement to work on his bike and avoid his father.

---

A few hours later, Jack and Amanda pulled into Austin's driveway in Jack's pickup.

Leaving the truck running, Jack hopped out and ran into the basement garage.

Austin's face was freshly bruised and dried blood clung to his nostrils. With no place left to escape, Austin had paid the price for motorcycles again.

Austin handed Jack the bottle. "Even?" Austin asked. He was tired of dealing with Jack and the increasing risks linked to it.

"The way I see it," Jack said as he stuffed the bottle down the front of his baggy pants, "vodka's pretty cheap rent for my old man. Since yours isn't worth a shit, I figure we ought to keep doing business. That is, if you still want to compete in Regionals."

Austin followed Jack outside and watched Jack and Amanda pull away in the brand new truck. Again, his life felt out of balance with the rest of the world.

Jack and Amanda left Austin's in search of a secluded spot to go parking. Out in the middle of nowhere, Jack pulled his truck off the main gravel road and onto a rough but secluded logging road. Amanda, sitting next to him, curled her left hand under his thigh and squeezed his leg. When Jack turned the truck off, she retrieved the bottle from under the seat and handed it to him.

Jack knew Austin watered down the vodka. Probably, he guessed, to keep from getting caught by his old man. He didn't really blame him and didn't really care. Half a bottle on

Saturday night was better than nothing.

Jack cracked the lid and took a quick gulp. He winced and looked at the bottle in disbelief. "This is straight stuff!"

"Cool," said Amanda.

Jack passed the bottle to Amanda then lit a bowl. He took a hit then traded with Amanda. For the better part of an hour, they drank, smoked, listened to tunes and kissed.

Feeling relaxed, comfortable and uninhibited, Jack laid Amanda down on the seat, unzipped her jeans and crawled on top of her. He knew what he wanted. What he needed. What she would provide.

"There's one left, isn't there?" Amanda casually reminded him. She enjoyed being the sole focus of his attention, even if it was only for a moment or two, but knew he wouldn't act responsibly on his own.

Jack begrudgingly opened the glove box and pulled out the last condom. With his arm under Amanda's neck, and the alcohol taking effect, he fumbled as he opened the package and dropped the contents into the dust on the floorboard.

"Oh, well," Jack said. "Where were we?" As he kissed her again, he reached down and brushed the condom under the seat.

## Chapter 10 – SECURITY

Spring was now in full swing and school would be over in less than two months. For Austin, the past six weeks had flown by. Regionals were just around the corner.

Austin, with his cast finally removed, worked with Gary on a Suzuki in the shop at Coast Range Cycle. Two technicians worked on two other bikes and a long line of bikes still waited to be repaired.

In the stockroom, Ben watched Jack count inventory. Ben could tell something was bothering Jack.

"You already got these?" Ben asked as he held up a box of very expensive VFORCE Reed Valves.

"Yeah," Jack said. Lost in his own thoughts, he barely paid attention to Ben or the inventory.

As Ben stuffed the box into the front pocket of his baggy jeans, they heard a light knock at the back door.

Without saying anything, Jack removed a plain box from the highest shelf and handed it to Ben. Ben removed half dozen dime bags of weed from the box and stuffed them in his other pocket. Jack put the box away and continued counting parts as Ben exited out the back door.

Outside, a man in a waiting car took the

pot and handed Ben a wad of folded bills.

"You almost done with that inventory, Jack?" Gary called out from the shop. "We could use an extra hand in here!"

Jack stomped into the shop and flung the handheld inventory recorder onto the counter. He snapped on blue nitrile mechanic's gloves. "I don't know why you promise everyone you'll have their bikes done by Friday!" Jack complained.

"Regional Qualifiers start in two weeks. They want track time and need their bikes to do it. Something you should think about," Gary answered.

"I don't need practice!" Jack's superior attitude was coming through loud and clear.

"Let me guess," Gary said, loosing his patience with Jack, "your bike doesn't need maintenance either?"

"You got it," Jack continued to push the envelope. "Why don't you help Austin here? You can practice being his dad some more."

The two technicians glanced at each other. Austin turned his head and kept working.

"Just get to work," Gary said, refusing to buy into Jack's foul mood. "Has Ben left yet?"

Jack nodded, "Yeah."

"Good," Gary said. "Maybe now I'll get some work out of you."

Later that day and still in a bad mood, Jack watched Austin pay Cindy for pants, matching jersey, boots, and a five-gallon can of race gas.

"Why don't you pick out a new pair of gloves?" Cindy asked Austin. "It's on me. Lord knows you've sold enough of them."

Fueled by a new set of problems, Jack subconsciously looked for a place to vent his fear, anger and frustration. His rising jealousy of Austin provided the perfect opening and his smart mouth quickly spiraled out of control.

"Why don't you just ask him to move in?" he sneered at his mom. "I can share my room!"

"You don't talk to me like that!" Cindy's usually sweet voice was instantly sharp and cutting. "Get out! Go home. Now!"

Jack stomped across the showroom and flung the front door open just as Ben walked up.

"Hey, the back door was locked," Ben said.

"Come on," Jack said.

Ben quickly turned around and followed Jack to his truck.

"Thanks anyway, Cindy," Austin answered as he watched the two of them peel out of the parking lot in Jack's truck. "I'll pass on the gloves. I'll get 'em next payday."

---

It was a gorgeous day when Gary pulled his trailer through the entrance of Clark's Ranch Motocross Park just outside of Roseburg, Oregon. A big sign read "Welcome Racers!" The outside temperature was right at eighty-five degrees, the sky was free of the standard heavy gray clouds and a slight breeze blew out of the south.

At the registration booth, Gary paid the entrance fees for Austin, Jack, and Ben.

The grounds literally buzzed with pre-race activity and excitement. Though not as nearly as big as Washougal, the track was still challenging. Plus, it was home to the first of the three regional qualifiers for the year.

Dressed in plain clothes, Gary waited outside the motorcycle trailer for the guys to change. Austin, Ben, and Jack emerged from the trailer dressed to race. Outfitted in his brand new gear, Austin looked like a totally different kid and a serious contender.

Amanda and Brooke, the makeshift pit crew and cheering section, walked up to the trailer and handed a Red Bull to each of them.

"Thanks girls," Gary said.

He turned to the guys. In a voice that was all business, he gave them a very to-the-point pep talk. "Listen up. There are two qualifiers after this. Place in the top 20 overall and you go to Regionals. The top four riders at Regionals go on to Nationals. You know what to do."

In Moto One, Jack blasted over the starting gate, made the holeshot and maintained his lead over Austin and Ben. Always right in front of Austin, Ben rode like he had a death wish and took incredible risks just to stay in his way.

Something didn't feel right to Austin. No matter how hard he tried, Austin couldn't pass

Ben. He hoped this race wasn't going to end like the last one. For Austin, this one was too important.

In Moto Two, Austin, Ben and Jack positioned their bikes against the starting line. It was a lucky break that Austin drew the treasured inside position. Everyone knew it was the only place to start in order to take the holeshot.

Jack leaned over his bike and looked at Austin. He grinned and flipped Austin off. Not quite sure where things stood between them, Austin weakly flipped him back.

When the flagman stepped onto the track, all the riders pulled their goggles into place, crouched down on their bikes and waited for that flag to drop. Austin dropped his head and said to himself, "My choice. My way."

Seconds ticked by. Austin memorized his line into the first corner and visualized the holeshot.

When the flag dropped, twenty riders blasted forward, but Jack took the lead, made the holeshot and blasted out of the first corner like a steel bearing released from a slingshot.

Through hairpin turns, rugged whoops and all the jumps, Jack held onto his lead even though Austin rode a tight second. Ben was right behind Austin and tried frantically to pass, but at each opportunity, Austin cut the corners tight and forced Ben to the outside. Ben stayed right behind Austin, but never managed to pass.

At the scoreboard, Gary watched a man mark numbers beside each name under the MOTO 2 category. MOTO 1 was already filled in with numbers from one to twenty. The few DNF's and DNS's were glaringly obvious. Usually because of stupid mistakes or tough breaks, the "did not finish" and "did not starts" were a frustrating waste of time and money to motocross riders.

Exhausted and covered with dirt, Austin, Ben and Jack joined Gary at the scoreboard right after the second race. In the columns beside Jack's name were "1" and "1". The man wrote a "2" in the FINAL column.

Beside Ben's name was "3" and "5". The man wrote an "8" in the FINAL column.

Austin read the numbers beside his name. He saw a "4", under Moto 1 and grinned as he watched the man write a "4" under the MOTO 2 column and an "8" in the FINAL column. Because their final score was tied and Austin had finished the second race ahead of Ben, Austin held 4th place and Ben was in 5th.

Ben kicked at the dirt with his motocross boot. He couldn't believe that Austin, sill riding his worn out bike, actually beat him.

"Thanks for the tip," Austin smiled at Gary.

"Looks like that race gas did the trick," Gary grinned back.

"That's the last time," Ben snapped at Jack as they stomped away from the sign.

# Chapter 11 –
## ATTENTION TO DETAIL

The following week was tense around the shop. Jack hardly spoke to Austin. Still recovering from his bruised ego, Ben didn't hang around as much, either.

Austin unpacked a shipment of gloves. He slid his hands into a large glove, made a fist then extended his fingers. The gloves fit well and were really comfortable. He was glad he had waited to buy a pair.

He hardly noticed when Cindy answered the ringing phone. She put the caller on hold and retrieved a bill from the office. Jack was busy keyboarding inventory data into the computer, but paid attention to the conversation.

"I'm saying you made a mistake," Cindy told the caller. "This medical bill isn't ours. Jack was in school."

Austin realized that Cindy was talking to the insurance company and walked over to Cindy.

"Capitates? Hamates? Metacarpals?" Cindy questioned the caller. "Look, I have no idea what you're talking about."

Austin looked at Cindy, who rolled her eyes and shook her head.

"It's your mistake. You fix it," Cindy demanded and abruptly hung up the phone.

"Cindy...um...well...there's something I should..." Austin stammered.

Just then, Gary walked up behind them carrying a stack of old inventory reports. Jack glared at Austin.

"Who was that on the phone?" Gary asked.

"The insurance company," Cindy said. "That's the second time they called about this bill. That should take care of it. What do you need, hon?"

"Would you pull the last two month's inventory reports? Something's out of whack. Inventory expense is up and purchases don't match sales." Gary was puzzled, but not too worried.

Cindy grinned and nodded at Jack. "I probably should have taught him how to count."

Jack wasn't in the mood to play. He was worried that Austin wouldn't keep his high-and-mighty mouth shut. He punched a key on the keyboard and sent the reports to the printer.

"What'cha need Austin?" Cindy turned her attention to Austin.

"Umm," Austin looked at Jack, who gave him that *don't you dare* look.

"Glove inventory is okay," Austin said.

---

Two weeks later, Gary pulled his truck and trailer through the main gate at Airway Heights Motocross Track in Washington for the second regional qualifier. Austin perked up and looked out the back seat window at the sign and the surroundings. Jack, in the front passenger seat, and Ben, in the back seat behind Gary, were both still asleep.

Because it was a five-hour drive from home, Amanda and Brooke opted out of their pit crew duties for the day. Amanda said she wasn't feeling well and Brooke had already promised her dad she would watch Bobby.

The track was smaller than the other tracks on the circuit and drew only a few spectators. It wasn't very congested with people or cars so it was easy to find parking in the pits. In no time, Jack and Ben stepped out of the trailer dressed in their motocross gear and were ready to race.

Also dressed and ready to go, Austin stood inside the trailer and quickly measured two-stroke oil and poured it into his orange plastic fuel jug. He had completely forgotten about it while they were loading up. He wished Brooke was here. She was good at remembering details like that. Austin added race gas up to the line, screwed on the lid, shook it gently, then set it on the floor next to the two other jugs, one blue, one red.

"Time to go, boys," Gary announced.

Austin, Jack and Ben were lined up at the starting gate with seventeen other riders. Grinning like a hyena, Ben flipped Austin off. Austin looked past him to Jack, who rubbed his eye with his middle finger, then slid his goggles in place. Austin didn't bother to respond and looked back at the track. He was tired of their juvenile games. He had one purpose for being here. Just one. Austin dropped his head.

Ben looked over at him. He could tell Austin was talking to himself. Ben smirked and said to himself, "All the prayers in the world won't help you today, loser."

Austin was ready and completely focused when the gate dropped. He screamed toward the corner ahead of Jack and cut him off. When Jack slowed down to keep from plowing into the berm, three more riders piled into him. No one was hurt and all four riders scrambled to get back on their bikes and back into the race.

Ben flew by the wreck hell-bent to catch Austin and bring him down, but Austin out-rode him at every turn, over the doubles and triples, and across each whoop.

When Austin flew across the finish line in first place, Ben was still right behind him. When Jack finished the race a few moments later, he went straight to the scoreboard and waited for the results.

At the scoreboard, Jack watched in disgust as the official mark a "13" next to his name name under MOTO 1. He couldn't believe he finished that far back.

Trying to beat the heat of the hot spring sun, Gary leaned against the shady side of the trailer and talked to Jack, who was agitated and angry.

It was difficult sometimes for Gary to balance the roles of coach and dad. As a coach, he knew Jack had the best resources of any rider in his class. On top of the latest equipment, he also had incredible skills and complete family support. Because of that, Gary felt Jack's potential was unlimited. But as the dad of an impatient and spoiled teenager, he feared Jack's cocky attitude might be his downfall.

Gary struggled to understand Jack's ambivalence. Because Gary's childhood had been more like Austin's, he vowed to be a better father and provide a good life for his son. As a result, Jack ended up with everything that Gary had always wanted as a kid. And unfortunately, Jack took it all for granted.

"No reason to get all upset. You'd have to DNF every race left to not make Regionals," Gary coached. "Relax. Just have fun."

Jack exchanged glances with Ben. "You're right, Dad. No big deal. Can we get something to eat?"

"Yeah, I'll be right back. Rest up for the last race," Gary said as he took off for the concession stand. He knew the girls were a distraction for the boys, but it was sure handy to have them around some of the time. Gary hated waiting in lines and would have gladly delegated the task of getting lunch to the girls.

Austin waved at Gary as he rode past him on his way to the trailer. Gary pointed to the concession stand and asked Austin in sign language if he wanted to eat. Austin nodded.

Jack leaned against the shady side of the trailer and scanned the crowd. Inside, Ben screwed the cap off a bottle of two-stroke oil.

When Austin rode up, Jack dropped his hand and knocked on the side of the trailer. Austin killed his bike and got off. Without a twinge of guilt, Ben stepped out of the trailer and closed the door behind him.

"Hey, Jack," Austin apologized. "Sorry about cutting you off."

"No problem," Jack replied. "It's all about having fun. Right, Ben?"

Austin looked from Jack to Ben, who wore a devilish grin. Something wasn't right. Austin hated the fact that he no longer trusted Jack, but he couldn't help it. They'd been good friends since kindergarten, but when they entered high school things changed - Jack started hanging around with Ben. By the time Jack was a senior he had turned into a cocky, arrogant, self-serving dick. Austin questioned why he still hung around him until he looked at his bike. That's why.

Austin opened the trailer door, grabbed his orange fuel jug and fueled up his bike. He finished just as Gary came back with a box filled with a forty-six dollar lunch: hot dogs loaded with chili, cheese and onions; four bags of potato chips; and four large soda pops.

In a rush to get out of the house before Steve woke up, Austin had skipped breakfast and was starving. At the time, racing was more important than food. But by now, even the overcooked and dried-out concession stand hotdogs smelled wonderful.

Gary handed each of the guys three dogs, a large bag of sour cream and onion potato chips, and a Coke. Delicious.

Later that day and back on the track for the second moto, Austin sat on his bike in the exact center of all the riders. This starting position usually led to a pile up in the first corner. Nevertheless, he focused his attention on the upcoming race and mentally selected his line. Without thinking, he revved his engine in anticipation. Jack and Ben glanced at each other but didn't bother with their traditional good luck signal. If Ben wanted to go to Nationals with Jack, they'd better get serious.

Crouched down in the ready position, Austin's concentration instantly evaporated the second he smelled it. Smoke poured from his bike like a chimney fire in an oil refinery. He turned to look at his muffler just as the gates dropped. With no time to think, Austin reacted and lurched off the line. A second later, his bike died. In a complete panic, he watched the other riders scream past him and stream through the corner.

Only ten feet in front of the gate, Austin frantically tried to kick-start his dead bike. He reached under and turned the fuel petcock. Kick. Kick. He switched to choke. Kick. Kick.

The engine gave nothing – except thick blue smoke from the exhaust.

Standing on the sidelines, Gary watched Austin get off his dead bike and silently push it toward the pits.

Later on at the scoreboard, Jack and Ben watched the Official mark a "1" next to Jack's name under Moto 2, a "3" next to Ben's and a "DNF" next to Austin's. They grinned as the official filled in the FINAL column. Jack "14", Ben "8", Austin "25".

---

At work on Monday, Austin examined new jets through their plastic wrap as he paid Cindy. Along with the jets, he bought a spark plug, two-stroke oil, race gas and a pair of those new gloves.

"Hey, thanks for the raise and the freestyle tickets," Austin said to Cindy. "You're not going?"

"I'd love to, but Gary and I made other plans," she answered. "Freestyle is fascinating. Need anything else for your bike?"

"This should do it," Austin said.

"Good luck next weekend at the last qualifier," Cindy said, as she looked cautiously around for Jack. When she saw that Jack was in the shop and out of earshot she added, "You're a good kid. You deserve to make it."

# Chapter 12 – TENACITY

Austin, dressed head to toe in his new race gear, pulled off his helmet and hung it on the bars. Sweat dripped off his forehead and mixed with the dust on his face. Brooke handed him a Red Bull and watched him gulp it down then wipe his mouth on his jersey sleeve. Back at the awesome Washougal track, Austin had completed his first moto for the last of the Regional Qualifiers.

"One down, one to go," Austin said.

"You're doing great!" Brooke said. "You're gonna make it to Regionals. I just know it."

"I need at least a ninth place finish to qualify. Better fuel up. Come with me?" Austin asked.

Brooke smiled warmly at him. She felt like she could follow him anywhere, but didn't want to come on too strong. Austin was very independent and, she figured, probably liked independent girls - not the high-maintenance and needy type.

"Sure," she said with a smile.

In the pits, Brooke and Austin were holding hands as they walked up to Gary's truck and trailer. Austin looked around nervously. No one was here. Gary was at the track with Jack, probably talking business with another dealer. Amanda didn't feel well enough to make the trip again, and Austin didn't know where Ben was.

Building his nerve, Austin turned and stepped closer to Brooke. He wanted to tell her how much he liked her, how much he appreciated her upbeat attitude. But all the words that came into his head seemed trite and cheesy.

So instead of hollow words, Austin leaned over to kiss her. For the first time, he looked directly into her blue-gray eyes, held his gaze, and smiled softly. He hesitated and looked at her lips. With perfect timing, they smiled back at him. He put his arm around her waist and pulled her toward him. When Austin's lips were only an inch away from Brooke's, he stopped and abruptly pulled back.

Still holding Brooke, he turned his head to listen. A noise came from inside the trailer. Austin looked at the door and saw that it was cracked open. Thinking something was getting ripped off, he let go of Brooke, walked over to the door and flung it open.

Caught off guard, Ben quickly dropped a bottle of two-stroke oil behind the fuel cans and stepped back.

"Oh...um...hey, how's it goin'?" Ben asked.

"What are you doing?" Austin was suspicious.

"Came back to get fuel. Just like you," Ben answered.

Ben tossed Austin the keys and quickly stepped out of the trailer with his blue fuel jug.

"Lock it, will ya?" Ben said as he walked away carrying his blue fuel jug.

Trying to figure out what Ben was up to, Austin looked from Ben, to Brooke, to the trailer. Austin opened the door wide and stepped in.

He looked around, noticed the open two-stroke oil bottle in the corner and jerked his orange fuel jug off the floor. Gas and oil spilled through the open lid. All of a sudden it clicked. He set the jug back down then picked up the empty two-stroke oil bottle and flung it back into the corner.

Ben had contaminated his fuel with extra two-stroke oil before the last moto at Airway Heights. No wonder his bike clogged up and died. And now, the extra fuel he needed for his last qualifying race was ruined. Austin picked up Jack's red fuel jug. It was already empty.

---

Back at the track, Brooke watched as Austin removed the gas cap on his bike and peered inside the plastic tank. He squatted down, shook the bike and looked at the low fuel level through the side.

"Is there enough?" Brooke asked.

"It's gonna be close. What if I DNF?" Austin said angrily. "This could be my last race!"

After a moment, Brooke said as calmly as she could, "then make it your best one."

Austin looked up at her. Her ability to turn a bad situation into something positive amazed him. She was all about choice. He liked that and nodded at her. "Yeah," he said. "I will. "

"And I'll wait for that kiss at the finish line," she smiled.

Racers rode their bikes onto the track and lined up at the starting gate. Once in place, they nervously revved their already warmed engines. To conserve as much fuel as possible, Austin pushed his bike into position and kept his eyes focused on the first corner.

Ben grinned at the whole drama. He was dying to see how it would all unfold and mouthed the word *loser* toward Austin. Jack tried to get Austin's attention and flip him off, but Austin ignored them.

In what seemed like a staged Hollywood production, the riders pulled their goggles into place in unison, ripped away tear-offs and crouched down to wait for the start. Seconds ticked by. Overflowing with adrenaline, Austin could hardly breathe as he waited for the moment.

When the official stepped up to the track, Austin quickly started his bike and let it run without twisting the throttle. Keeping his eyes wide open and on the official at all times, Austin said to himself, "My choice. My way."

Finally, the race gates dropped. Like an innocent prisoner bolting for freedom, Austin jetted past the gates and took off for the holeshot.

Hugging the dirt on the inside of the first corner, Austin narrowly squeezed into the lead. He knew it was time to risk it all.

Through hairpin turns, rugged whoops, the rhythm section, and over all of the double and triple jumps, Austin hung onto his precious narrow lead. Nearing the end of the race, Austin cut the tightest corner on the track so close that Jack had no choice but to take the outside or wreck.

When Austin saw the checkered flag waving at the finish line just beyond the whoops, he headed into them full throttle. Like a drag racer on the salt flats, his front wheel never touched the ground. Still, Jack was right on his tail.

Even though Brooke knew Austin couldn't pick her out of the crowd, she cheered him on at the finish line.

With only one whoop left in front of him, Austin was close to his first win! Even if Jack managed to pass him now, Austin would still finish in second place and make the cut.

Brooke could barely contain her excitement. She screamed, cheered and clapped until her hands were red and sore.

Suddenly, Austin's bike sputtered. Instinctively, he gassed it, but it sputtered again, died and instantly lost momentum. His fuel was gone. In a blur, Jack flew past him and crossed the finish line in first place.

Austin jumped off his dead bike and pushed it over the last whoop and ran all out toward the waving flag.

Brooke screamed, "COME ON! Keep going! You can do it!"

The spectators roared as two more riders screamed by Austin. Brooke pushed her way to the front of the crowd and screamed his name. He heard her and saw her hold up her fingers. Four. Five. Watching the track behind him, she frantically waved him on then held up her fingers as two more riders passed. Six! Seven! Only a few yards to go. "Come on Austin!" Brooke screamed, "Run!"

Another rider flew past him in a blur. At a dead run and still pushing his bike through the soft, fluffy dirt, Austin looked up quickly at Brooke. Through splattered goggles, he saw her hold up eight fingers. He had to come in ninth place to qualify. Austin heard another bike behind him at the same instant Brooke saw it.

Austin fought to breathe through his clenched teeth as he pushed his bike across the finish line just in time. Finishing only seconds ahead of the next racer, he had his ninth place!

He quickly pushed the bike off the track and out of the way of the other racers. Still holding onto the bars, he fell over the seat and tried to catch his breath. Brooke ran over to him, draped her arms over his back and squeezed him.

"Congratulations! You did it!" she said.

Still breathing hard, Austin laid his bike on its side and peeled off his helmet. Holding his helmet in his right hand, he grabbed Brooke around the waist and pulled her in tight with his left arm. All sweaty and dusty, and in front of a huge, cheering crowd, he kissed her.

"Thank you," he said quietly and smiled.

"Anytime," Brooke smiled back.

Austin handed Brooke his helmet and picked up his bike. "Now, where's Ben?"

## Chapter 13 – ACCOUNTABILITY

Brooke carried Austin's helmet and walked beside him as he pushed his bike back to the pits. Jack was in the cab of the truck with his head in his hands.

"You seen Ben?" Austin asked through the open cab window.

"Why?" Jack lifted his head and smiled.

"Because that moron dumped oil in my fuel and almost cost me the race," Austin barked as he pushed his bike to the back of the trailer.

"Almost? What?" Jack said.

Just then, Ben rode up and killed his bike. Without looking at Austin or Brooke, he pulled out the ramp and started to load his bike. Austin propped his bike against the trailer and strutted up to Ben.

"Think you wouldn't get caught, asshole?" Austin demanded.

"What are you talking about?" Ben asked, keeping his motorcycle between himself and Austin.

Austin leaned over the bike, got in Ben's face and punched a finger into his shoulder. "I'm talking about you putting oil in my fuel like you did at Airway Heights!"

Jack got out of the truck and walked to the back of the trailer.

"Prove it," Ben said.

"I don't need proof! I saw you do it!"

"I think Austin's callin' you a liar, Ben," Jack pressed.

"You want a piece of me too, Jack? Go ahead. Take the first swing!" Austin spread his arms wide. "Bring it on."

"What's going on?" Gary came around from the other side of the trailer.

"You saw it. My bike died on the finish line, just like it did at Airway Heights. Brooke and I saw Ben coming out of the trailer. The lid was off my fuel and an empty two-stroke bottle was thrown in the corner.

"Umm...I left that one there, Dad," Jack covered for Ben. "I was in a hurry."

"Look, Austin. Your bike is old. It's not going to run perfectly all the time," Gary said. "You should be happy right now. You qualified for Regionals!"

Jack was stunned. He didn't know.

"Yeah, but just barely," Austin said. "It was way too close!"

"Let it go, Austin," Brooke said. "Things like this have a way of working out. You'll see."

## Chapter 14 – GROWTH

Brooke and Amanda sipped sodas at Pizza in Paradise secluded in a bright red booth with tall backs. Trying to keep their conversation from being overheard, they kept their voices hushed.

"Have you told your folks yet?" Brooke asked.

"No, just you and Jack," Amanda answered. "And his parents don't know yet either. They're all gonna freak."

"What did Jack say?"

"That he doesn't want to think about it until after Nationals."

"Well, *you've* got three choices then," Brooke said. "There was a fourth one."

"What?" Amanda asked desperately.

"Prevention!" Brooke said sternly. She had a hard time understanding how Amanda could have been so reckless.

"Shut up, you prude! You sound like the school counselor. I don't need a lecture right now. I need help deciding what to do," Amanda said.

"I'm not a prude. I don't have a problem with you and Jack having sex. Or anybody else for that matter. It's about birth control," Brooke said. "I thought you were on the pill."

"I never thought it would happen to me," Amanda was near tears.

"It's a tough decision," Brooke sighed. "One that will affect the rest of your life, no matter what you choose."

Amanda looked at Brooke and rolled her eyes. "Like I don't know that?"

Brooke realized the mistake of thinking out loud and tried to soften the conversation a little. "Look, I'm sorry. I didn't mean it like that. Try to see it this way," Brooke said. "You're already eighteen and at least you're graduating. Most of girls that get pregnant in high school never finish. You still have choices. You can still work or go to college."

"You don't get it, do you?" Amanda was frustrated. "I had my life all planned out. Jack is going to win Nationals and we're going to move to California when Jack picks up a Factory Ride. How would it look at the races for me to be lugging a baby around? It's Jack's career that's important. Not mine."

Brooke couldn't believe what she was hearing. "How can you say that what Jack wants is more important than what you want?"

"Because it is. I love him," Amanda said.

"You think he feels loved right now?" Brooke quipped, unable to hold back the sarcasm. "My guess is he feels trapped."

---

Two weeks later on a hot June afternoon, Gary and Cindy sat next to Steve in the high school auditorium and listened to Austin, the class Valedictorian, give a short speech to his three hundred classmates and their families. Wearing traditional burgundy cap and gowns, everyone, including Austin, was anxious to get the graduation ceremony over with.

"In closing," Austin said quickly, "I'd like to share with you what a good friend recently told me. She said that our lives are just a series of choices." He paused for a moment. "Make good ones. Thank you." Set apart from his peers by the gold collar and tassel, Austin left the podium under a round of raucous applause.

Sitting with friends in the crowd, Brooke smiled and cheered. She was proud to be his girlfriend.

The other students, including Ben, Jack and Amanda, whose pregnancy was starting to show, followed Austin across the stage one at a time and received their scrolled diplomas. This phase of their lives was finally over. And, whether they liked it or not, it was time to move on.

# Chapter 15 – JUDGEMENT

Heavy bass and pulse-pounding music poured out of the huge Rose Garden Arena in Portland, Oregon when Austin opened the heavy glass door for Brooke. Sporting new clothes and a haircut, Austin was thrilled to be on his first official date with her.

Hundreds of vendors lined the wide arena hallways and sold t-shirts, hats, videos, posters and anything else that touted the latest Freestyle stars and their company sponsors.

At a vendor's table, Austin stopped and bought a Freestyle video and handed it to Brooke. "A token of our first date," he grinned. Brooke smiled and put the video into her purse.

After stopping for a soda, Brooke and Austin found their seats in a packed house. On the dirt-covered arena floor, two huge, steep ramps loomed at each end. Competitors dressed in brightly colored motorcycle gear circled the ramps and warmed up for the upcoming freestyle competition.

"These are great seats!" Brooke said as they sat down. "Which one is Ben?"

"Over there in the blue jersey." Austin pointed him out. Ben circled the competition area on a Yamaha.

"How come he's not riding his KTM?" she asked.

"Because he's an idiot," Austin said.

"What?" Brooke laughed.

"Just kidding," Austin grinned, trying to camouflage his still-bitter feelings about Ben. "His KTM is geared for motocross. Different sports need different tools. Watch. You'll see."

The emcee's voice boomed and echoed over the speaker system. "Welcome ladies and gentlemen to the Freestyle Motocross Competition in Portland, Oregon!" At that moment, the music intensified and the crowd became part of the beat. Part of the action. Brooke and Austin cheered and clapped along with everyone else.

"Tonight ladies and gentlemen," the emcee continued, "the riders are competing for a twenty-five thousand dollar first prize! Ten thousand dollars for second place and five thousand dollars for the third place finisher!" The crowd cheered. "So, sit back and hold on tight, because these boys won't be!"

Austin took hold of Brooke's hand and smiled at her. Together they watched as a rider left the launch pad, charged up the ramp and sailed into midair fifty feet above the dirt covered arena floor.

"It's Superman!" the emcee announced, his big voice echoing through the arena like a chorus of gods.

At the top of the arc, the rider pulled the bike toward his body, placed his hips near the handlebars, then straightened out his arms and kicked his feet back at the same time. Flying through the air parallel with the bike, the rider looked like Superman. Once the trick was completed, the rider quickly got back on the bike and coasted smoothly down the other ramp. It was spectacular.

Never having been to a freestyle competition, Brooke watched in awe and amazement. "How in the world can they do that? It looks impossible!" she squealed.

"They used to say that about skateboards too," Austin said. "It's just physics - momentum, angles and gravity. And, like any other sport, lots of practice."

Another rider soared off the ramp and momentarily disappeared behind the hanging scoreboard. Once in the air, he performed the "Catwalk". The rider threw both of his legs to one side of the bike and moved them rapidly back and forth, like he was walking. The stunt took only a few seconds, then the rider got back on the bike and made the smooth landing look easy.

"The Catwalk!" the emcee's voice boomed.

One right after another, the riders performed for the cheering crowd. Each stunt was more and more complicated and increasingly dangerous.

An eager young rider whipped out a "Kiss of Death". The rider extended his body over the handlebars, perpendicular to the bike, and kissed the front fender. Barely leaving enough time to get back on the seat, the rider wobbled and almost went down on the landing.

Brooke inhaled rapidly. "Ohh..!"

"That was almost a real Kiss of Death!" the emcee roared. His voice grew more excited with each near miss. "Coming up next," he teased the crowd, "the one...the only...the Backflip!"

Ben waited at the top of the launching ramp for the all-clear signal.

"Ben can't do a Backflip!" Austin gasped. "Jack said he crashed the only time he tried it on his track! What the heck is he thinking?"

Ben roared up the ramp, pumped the bike and pulled back. He circled through the air upside down then pulled the bike toward him. The crowd never stopped cheering.

Almost over and leveling out, Ben stood straight up on the pegs and got ready to land. Suspended in anticipation, twenty-five thousand spectators watched as Ben soared toward the landing ramp on the arena floor. But, in what seemed like slow motion, Ben overshot the ramp and landed brutally hard. As a result, both of his legs bowed grotesquely outward, then snapped in painful unison just before the momentum blasted him and the bike violently into the wall. He collapsed into an unconscious, tangled heap at the bottom of it.

Brooke covered her mouth with her hand. The entire arena became instantly silent. For a second, everything stopped.

Paramedics rushed over to Ben, carefully

strapped him to a backboard and loaded his limp body onto a gurney. Just before he was put into the ambulance, Ben's arm flopped off his chest and dangled over the side. Even thought his eyes were still closed, he managed a weak wave to the crowd.

"Looks like he's going to make it," the emcee reported. "A little banged up, but okay. Let's hear a big round of applause for Ben Wilson!" The crowd applauded and cheered.

"This is crazy!" Brooke gasped. "Is he going to be okay?"

Austin just shrugged.

"Why do guys do this?" Brooke asked in disbelief.

"Adrenaline! It's all about the rush," Austin smiled. Austin understood it perfectly, but Brooke wasn't convinced.

She smiled back at Austin. "There are other ways to get a rush, you know."

---

Back at his house, Austin held the front door open for Brooke. He quietly carried a grocery bag to the table and unloaded a six-pack of soda and a box of microwave popcorn.

Brooke looked at the clock. It wasn't quite midnight. Enjoying the freedom of summer vacation, she had slept in that morning and was still wide awake. She pulled the video from her purse and read the jacket.

Steve stumbled out of the bathroom carrying a drink and saw Brooke. "Who's this?" he slurred.

Caught off guard and startled, Brooke stepped closer to Austin.

"This is my girlfriend, Brooke," Austin answered.

"Hi," Brooke said hesitantly.

"Yeah," Steve mumbled.

Austin opened the box of microwave popcorn, turned toward the empty spot on the counter and stopped mid-movement.

"Dad, where's the microwave?" Austin asked.

"Nick's got it down at the shop," Steve said.

Austin noticed that Steve's watch was missing from his wrist and dropped his head in disbelief. "I didn't know it was *that* broke," Austin replied sarcastically.

"I'll pick it up when I get paid," Steve said. "Gonna hit the sack." Still carrying his drink, Steve wobbled back down the hall.

Austin watched him leave then stared blankly at the popcorn box.

Brooke took the box from his hand and pull out a package of popcorn. "How about a pan with a lid," she said. Without judgment and without blame, she just calmly and easily solved the problem.

When the popcorn was ready, Austin put the Freestyle tape into the VCR and sat down on the couch. Brooke put the pan of popcorn on the floor next to them.

Facing the TV, Austin and Brooke laid on the couch and snuggled. Stretched out and relaxed, Austin propped his head up with one hand and draped the other one over Brooke's slender waist.

When the video was over, Austin reached over Brooke and picked up a single piece of popcorn from the pan. Without taking his eyes from the TV, he tried to put it into her mouth. She smiled when he missed and smeared butter on her nose. He tried again and smeared butter on her cheek.

Laughing, Brooke rolled over and looked at him. In good-natured defeat, he held the piece of popcorn up to her mouth. She took hold of it with her lips, then lifted her head closer to him. Austin leaned over, took the popcorn from her lips with his, and kissed her in between smiling and chewing.

Ignoring the leftover popcorn and the bright blue television screen, Brooke and Austin kissed until the gray light of dawn. For one brilliant evening, Austin's world was finally right.

## Chapter 16 – RECOGNITION

In the middle of another busy day, Gary finally found a spare moment to make an overdue and important phone call. He'd been meaning to get around to it for two weeks, but business was especially brisk this summer. And deep down, he wasn't sure how the conversation would go.

"Hi Steve, Gary here," he said. He listened for a second then continued. "I'm good, thanks. Say, listen. Would you mind stopping at the shop after work today?" Gary paused. "There's something I think you should know about," Gary continued. "Great. See you then."

Just before closing time that day, Austin was talking with his last customer when he saw Steve walk in. Austin noticed immediately that Steve's watch was back on his wrist. Paydays were a mixed blessing.

Instantly anxious, Austin eyes shifted rapidly between his customer, his dad, and Gary. He wished he could hear their conversation. Just once he'd like to look at his father without his preconditioned fear rising to the surface.

"Hey Austin. Got a minute?" Gary called to him from across the room.

"Would you excuse me for a moment?" Austin asked his customer., who nodded.

Now Austin knew the conversation was

about him. Guilt rose instantly to the forefront of his thoughts. As he walked across the showroom floor, the possibilities flashed in his mind like the lightening just before a tornado. Stealing parts? Broken hand? Racing? Vodka for Jack? Austin's heart rate increased and pounded with each step that took him closer to Gary and his dad. Right. Ba-boom. Left. Ba-boom. Once again, Austin felt that sickening sense of impending doom and embarrassment.

Austin could scarcely breathe as he stood next to them. He watched as Gary pulled an envelope from his shirt pocket and handed it to Steve.

"This is for you," Gary said to Steve.

Steve looked inside the envelope then looked up at Gary and Austin with an expression Austin had never seen on his dad's face before now. Just for an instant, a fraction of a second, Austin saw fear. Pure and terrifying. Just like his own. Austin stood motionless and waited.

"Tickets for Washougal tomorrow," Gary explained. "Austin made it to Regionals! It'd be like old times! What do you say?"

Suddenly, Steve lurched toward Austin. Instinctively, Austin flinched but Steve grabbed hold of him, gave him an awkward hug and a hard slap on the back. "He didn't tell me!" Steve forced excitement into his voice. "Congratulations, Austin! Yeah, sure, what the heck."

Feeling uncomfortable and vulnerable, Austin quickly pulled back and grinned half-heartedly. "Uh...well...I'd better get back to my customer," Austin stammered. "Thanks Gary." Austin walked back to the showroom and went back to work. Still trembling, he picked up where he left off with his customer, but continued to watch Steve and Gary.

When Gary shook his hand, Steve smiled warmly and thanked him. As Steve turned around and headed for the door, Austin saw the smile on his dad's face instantly evaporate. The charade was over. When Steve passed him on his way out, Austin felt that old, familiar anger already boiling inside his father.

"See you tonight, kid."

Austin dropped his head. Here we go again.

---

The next day, Gary drove his truck and trailer up the narrow entrance road past signs that read "Northwest Region Motocross Competition" and "Washougal MX Park". As he looked for a place to park in the crowded pits, Gary drove past the KTM factory semi truck. Austin rubbernecked at their awesome display of bikes, team posters and trophies - all under a huge orange awning.

"Everybody that is anybody is here today," Gary said. "Scouts, sponsors, factory reps, you name it. You want to get noticed, this is the place to start."

As soon as Gary turned off the diesel engine, the boys piled out and unloaded their bikes.

Amanda pulled Ben's pickup into the space next to them. Gary unloaded Ben's four-wheeler from the back of his pickup just as Brooke showed up.

Dressed in sexy summer clothing, Brooke leaned against the shady side of the trailer next to Amanda, who was now obviously pregnant and uncomfortable in the heat. From now on, looking sexy would be the last thing on her mind.

Permanently done with racing, Ben sat on a four-wheeler with crutches threaded through the handlebars. Both of Ben's legs were casted below the knee. He was still angry that Austin had made it to Regionals. It should have been just him and Jack, like last year.

Inside the trailer, Jack and Austin changed into their motocross gear. Jack pulled his silver jersey over his head as Austin quickly peeled off his t-shirt. Hoping to get his jersey on before Jack noticed, he quickly pushed his head through the neck opening.

"Damn! What happened to you?" Jack said as he looked at Austin's chest and back. It was covered with bruises, some old, some new.

Brooke quickly looked into the trailer. Austin discreetly shook his head to silence her and finished putting his jersey on.

"Motocross is a dangerous sport, right Ben?" Austin called outside, trying to divert Jack's attention.

"Screw you," Ben snarled back.

"Shut up, Ben," Brooke openly defended Austin. "Your stupidity isn't his fault. What goes around comes around, remember?"

Austin emerged from the trailer dressed for battle. He looked like a champion and he could tell that Brooke was proud of him. Austin glowered at Ben then handed his orange fuel jug to Brooke.

"Thanks babe," he said, then kissed her.

"Fourth or better," Brooke said like it was already front page news. "You can do it."

Austin and Jack pulled on their helmets, started their bikes then rode to the track. Amanda hopped on the four-wheeler behind Ben. Brooke, carrying Austin's fuel jug, was content to walk alone.

At the track, Ron Heben stood next to Bill Mitchell and waited for everything to play out. They watched as the riders pulled up to the starting gate.

Across the track, Steve waited with Gary. "Glad you could make it. Seems like just yesterday we were out there," Gary reminisced.

Steve didn't respond. He was extremely uncomfortable. Watching Austin race was the hardest thing he had done in thirty years. His mental anguish teetered on the sharp edge between excruciating and intolerable. He didn't know if he could hack it.

Gary noticed Steve's uneasiness, but the revving engines on the starting line drew his attention to the start of the first 250 moto.

The second the gates hit the ground, Jack screamed off the line toward the first corner and made the holeshot. After a slow start, Austin came out of the corner in tenth position. Stuck in the middle of the pack, he knew he had a lot of ground to make up.

In the first lap of the race, Jack rode brilliantly and maintained his lead. Determined to catch him, Austin rode aggressively but smart. Passing the other riders on the most technical part of the track, he managed to hold onto his gain even on the steep up-hills.

Steve watched Austin, who was gaining on Jack, explode off the last whoop and speed away from them toward the finish line. Like a shotgun blast to the gut, Steve's flashback hit him again. Everything in front of him flashed white.

Once again, in Steve's tortured, hazy-yellow memory, a 1970's motocross racer, in Austin's exact image, sped away from him toward a stand of fir trees that lined the track. In his vision, the rider hit the outside corner of the berm head on and bounced wildly off the track toward the trees.

When the crowd roared, Steve snapped back to reality. Ben, Amanda and Brooke cheered when Jack, on his way to the finish line, performed a freestyle whip over the last jump in front of the grandstand.

Steve glanced sideways at Gary, who was absorbed in the race, then covertly tried to shake the vision from his head.

Up ahead, the checkered flag waved wildly. Acting like the professional for once, Jack never let up and screamed his bike across the finish line in first place. Another rider took a close second and Austin followed in third place. The rest of the pack roared across the line seconds behind him.

Riding back to the pits with Jack, Austin saw Steve walking through the crowd. He thought about going over to him in spite of their recent fight, but hesitated. Subconsciously, Austin wanted and needed his father's approval, but he also hated him. When Austin saw Steve take a drink from a quart of orange juice, he decided to follow Jack back to the trailer. Better to leave that monster bottled up.

The two racers coasted up to the trailer and killed their bikes. They peeled off their helmets and goggles and wiped their sweaty faces with wet shop towels. Racing was an incredibly strenuous workout, especially on a hot day.

Brooke met Austin at the trailer with a bottle of water, which he downed in seconds. Without saying a word, she smiled her approval, handed him his orange fuel jug and stood by while he refueled.

Gary walked up just as Amanda and Ben pull up on the four-wheeler.

"Bikes running okay?" he asked as he visually inspected the bikes.

"So far so good," Austin said confidently.

Gary nodded then spoke to Jack, "Change your chain. It's worn out. There's a new one in the trailer."

Jack bent down and lifted up his chain. It was loose and a little worn, but not that bad.

"It's fine. It'll make one more race," Jack said, then turned his attention to his pregnant girlfriend. "Let's get something to drink."

As Jack and Amanda walked toward the concession stand, Gary looked at the chain. He wanted the best for his son. He knew the chain was worn out and thought about changing it himself. Gary looked at Austin, who waited to see what he would do.

At this moment, Gary felt completely torn. He knew that Austin would have listened to his advice and replaced the chain. If he replaced the chain for Jack, who was too lazy to do it himself, Austin would feel like he was choosing sides. Technically, Coast Range Cycle sponsored both of them.

Gary looked at Austin in bewilderment then shook his head. Jack wasn't a little boy anymore. He was finished with high school. It was time he grew up and took responsibility for his own destiny, his own life. Still, the tough love part of being a parent was hard for him.

"Well, it's his choice," Gary said. "I'll never understand why some kids have to learn the hard way."

Over at the concession booth, Jack bought a Red Bull for himself and a bottle of water for Amanda. As they left the booth, they passed Austin and Brooke, who were heading for the factory trucks.

"You really ought to change that chain, Jack," Austin said as he kept walking.

Jack didn't even acknowledge them.

"There's your dad," Brooke said and pointed at Steve going into the porta-potty.

Austin put his arm over Brooke's shoulder and pulled her in the opposite direction. She wrapped her arm around his waist and squeezed his ribs. Austin winced.

"Careful," he said.

"Sorry. I forgot," Brooke answered.

"It's okay. C'mon." Austin had more important things to think about.

Austin and Brooke walked up to the KTM factory semi and looked at the gleaming bikes. They were awesome. Brand new and state-of-the-art, they had all the best after-market parts. Austin knew that he could be so much better on a decent machine. He looked over at Ron, who sat at a table and signed autographs with the KTM Pro Team. Brooke looked at Austin. She could tell he wanted to talk to him.

"Go on," Brooke said. "You have one life. Make it the best one."

Austin took a deep breath and walked over to the table. He stuck his hand out at Ron and held eye contact.

"Hi. I'm Austin Davis. Number two eighty-seven."

Ron stood up, shook his hand and smiled at him.

"Ron Heben. Right, I remember. The Rainbow Rider. How's the hand?"

"Good as new," Austin said as he turned his hand over and around. "Thanks. Can I ask you a question?"

"Sure. Fire away," Ron said.

"What do I have to do to make your team?" Austin said, his words coming across more like a statement than a question.

Ron grinned. He had watched Austin and knew what he, and the millions like him, needed to hear. "Give it your best," Ron said. "Go for the win."

The other KTM riders smiled at his answer. They had all heard the same statement at one time or another.

"We'll save you a place," one of the Factory Riders smiled.

Austin grinned. "Thanks. I'll give it all I've got."

---

Austin and Brooke walked back to the trailer. The doors were wide open and they could hear someone inside mixing fuel. Austin quickly looked around for his fuel jug then remembered where he put it. He rushed over to the truck to see if it was still locked inside. It was.

He poked his head into the trailer and saw Gary mixing Jack's fuel. "Wait out here just a second?" Austin asked Brooke.

She nodded as Austin stepped inside. Brooke leaned against the trailer then suddenly lurched forward when her back touched the hot metal siding.

"Got a minute?" Austin asked Gary.

"Sure. What'cha need?" Gary replied.

"The keys to the truck?" Austin asked.

Gary reached into his pocket and handed Austin the keys. Austin hesitated for a moment.

"Gary, I want to say thanks for all you've done. I wouldn't be where I am if it weren't for you."

"Ah, it's just good business," Gary said then added, "You're welcome."

"Jack's lucky to have such a great dad," Austin said.

They smiled at each other - the kind of smile that said more than words possibly could.

Resting in the shade on the opposite side of the trailer, Steve listened to their conversation. The words that spilled so easy from Austin's mouth were like acid to his ears.

Steve knew that Austin didn't look to up to him, idolize him or even respect him. With sudden and unexpected clarity, Steve realized for the first time that he was losing his son. Before long, he'd be completely alone. Then what?

That thought pushed him closer to the edge of the dark hole that called out to what little there was left of his soul. Still clutching his bottle of orange juice and vodka, Steve stumbled to his truck in the parking lot and drove away.

---

The race that determined whether Austin's dream for Nationals would come true or not was next. Refreshed and ready for the second moto, Austin strapped on his helmet and pulled up next to Jack at the starting gate. Gary gave them both thumbs up. Jack tipped his helmet. Austin took a deep breath.

Austin found Ron standing on the sidelines and gave him a nod. Ron didn't visibly respond, but kept his eye on Austin and watched as he lowered his head.

"My choice. My way," Austin whispered.

Through his goggles, Austin watched the starting gates drop. Throttle pinned, he exploded away in first gear, then second, clutch, back brake, sharp left turn. In a furious battle for position, Austin made the holeshot and escaped with a lead of only a few inches.

Neck and neck, Jack and Austin competed fiercely through the entire grueling course. They took turns leading and passing each other, each needing the win for a different reason.

Never letting up, not once, Austin rode with all the grit he possessed. All the anger, all the hatred and all the resentment that he had suffered and stuffed down over the years was allowed freedom and vehemently channeled into winning this race. He knew the checkered flags that beckoned him had the power to change lives. To change his life.

Austin focused on the track just in front of his bike as he screamed through a hairpin turn. Once out of the turn, he quickly looked back at the track and, from the corner of his goggles, saw his roostertail land on Jack, who was right behind him.

Austin twisted the throttle and jetted off the berm only to be passed by Jack again on the straightaway. As Austin started into the whoops, he was only a bike-length behind Jack. Evenly matched, their back tires skimmed the tops off every other whoop.

On the last whoop before going into the final lap, Jack's back wheel slammed down hard and the weak chain snapped. Propelled by the momentum of the back sprocket, the chain spun off and sailed through the air like a poisonous water snake swimming against a turbulent current.

In what felt like slow motion, Austin watched the chain coming straight for him. Instinctively, he crouched down on his bike. The end of the chain grazed his goggles then whipped a slice into the top of his helmet. Austin's head snapped back as the chain ricocheted through the air then landed in the dust.

As Jack's bike rolled to a dead stop, Austin quickly looked back and realized that he was now in the lead with only one lap to go. He gassed it and sailed high over the jump in front of the grandstand.

The crowd that had falsely anticipated the outcome of the race became re-energized. Suddenly, everyone was rooting for the underdog. For Austin. And he could feel it.

With renewed enthusiasm, but guarded confidence, Austin assaulted the last lap. The exhaustion in his muscles vanished as his focus shifted. Instead of trying to catch the guy in front of him, he was now running from the riders behind him. But, the track ahead of him was clear. With no one in his way and the air free of dust, racing suddenly entered a new dimension. Leading the race was much better than being part of the pack. It felt right.

Austin flew over the finish line and passed the waving checkered flag several bike lengths ahead of his closest competitor. He slowed his bike down, shifted into second gear and started to exit the track. An official quickly motioned for him in the other direction. For a second Austin was confused. The official pointed at the checkered and gestured another lap with his hand. Austin grinned as he realized that, for the first time at Washougal, he got to ride the victory lap.

When he rode past the stand, he saw Brooke cheering and bouncing nearly out of control. When Austin blew her a kiss, she pretended to faint. Her animated antics and enthusiasm made Austin smile.

He nodded at Ron and waved at Gary. Austin looked around for his dad, but couldn't find him in the crowd.

After his victory lap, Austin quickly joined Gary and Jack at the scoreboard and watched as the official marked place numbers for Moto Two. Moto One was already filled in. As usual, a few DNF's and DNS's littered the board.

Ron stood behind the crowd at the scoreboard and recorded the final scores on his palm pilot.

In the columns beside Jack's name was a number one and a DNF. The Official wrote 17 in the final's column. Jack kicked at the dirt as he left. He couldn't believe it. Only the top four went to Nationals and he wasn't even close.

"Thanks for changing my chain, Dad," Jack sneered as he walked passed his father.

The official dropped down to the next racer's line and wrote a three in the Moto Two column, then filled in the final's column. The rider groaned in the background. He had missed his shot at Nationals by only one place.

Austin read the numbers beside his name – Moto One: Three. Moto Two: One. As the official wrote a four under the Final's column, Austin grinned ear to ear. He made it.

Gary slapped him affectionately on the back and said, "Way to go, kid. You worked hard for that one. You deserve it!"

A few seconds later, Ron walked up to Austin and shook his hand. "Congratulations," Ron said. "That was a great race. I'll look for you at Nationals."

## Chapter 17 – HUMOR

It was a special occasion and Brook's treat. Seated in the back booth at Paradise Pizza, Austin and Brooke finished their last bites of barbecue chicken pizza while they waited for the server to refill their sodas. The server returned and placed two more cherry cokes and a packet of matches on the table. As the server walked away, she nodded and smiled mischievously at Brooke.

"Thanks," Brooke smiled back at her. She looked at Austin with raised eyebrows, but said nothing.

Austin watched curiously as Brooke finally opened the brown paper grocery bag that had sat beside her undisturbed for the entire evening. Brooke reached into the bag, retrieved a large poppyseed muffin and placed it on the empty aluminum pizza tray.

Teasing Austin with intentional delays, she took her time getting another muffin out of the bag. After she placed it next the first one, she pulled out a can of whipped cream and shook it gently.

Austin sensed that the other customers in the restaurant were trying to look into their booth. He glanced around, shifted uncomfortably, but started to laugh when Brooke covered the muffins in whipped cream.

Not wanting to draw further attention from

the other customers, Austin covered his mouth to stifle his laughter.

When Brooke fished a cherry out of each of their cokes and splashed soda on the table, Austin laughed harder.

Keeping her cool, Brooke opened a box of birthday candles and stuck one candle through each of the cherries then into the center of each muffin.

By this time, Austin was laughing uncontrollably. Deep laughter that felt more like crying washed over Austin in waves as giddy tears ran down his face.

"Happy eighteenth," Brooke grinned at him.

Austin couldn't believe it. His birthday cake looked like two huge breasts. It was hardly the type of cake he remembered as a little boy, but it was the only birthday cake he'd had since his mother left for California six years ago. He loved it.

People in the restaurant continued to stare their direction, which only made them both laugh harder. As much as they tried, they couldn't stop giggling. Like two misbehaving children in church, Austin and Brooke laughed until their sides ached.

For both of them, the rest of the evening would be a night they would always remember.

# Chapter 18 – ALLEGIANCE

It was Monday morning at Coast Range Cycle. The start of a new workweek, a new month and the beginning of a new era in Austin's life. Today, he felt like a different person. Like a man.

Winning the race at Regionals and qualifying for Nationals was only part of it. His relationship with Brooke was most of it. He felt good about her. Really good.

Jack interrupted Austin's pleasant thoughts as he walked behind the service counter and shoved some paperwork at Austin.

"Here! Read this," Jack demanded as he watched Amanda, dressed in a large maternity top and shorts, storm out the front doors. Jack was glad she was leaving.

Austin took the paperwork and quickly scanned through the pages as Jack paced behind him.

"What's that all about?" Ben asked as he hobbled closer on his crutches.

"Punch some numbers in for me," Austin said as he tossed a calculator to Ben.

"Three hundred seventy-five dollars," Austin said.

Balancing on his crutches, Ben plugged in the numbers.

"Times twelve months. Times eighteen years," Austin said. "What's the total?"

"Eighty-one thousand," Ben said, still not understanding the significance.

Austin whistled loudly. Even he couldn't believe it was that much.

"Eighty-one THOUSAND dollars!" Austin gasped. "That's one expensive ride. Hope she was worth it!"

"What are you talking about?" Ben still didn't get it.

"The price tag for a bad split-second decision," Austin said, shaking his head in amazement.

"What?" Ben was brain-dead.

"Child support, you idiot!" Jack yelled.

---

Later that morning, Jack counted inventory in the stock room. Still angry, he aggressively pulled parts off the shelves, counted them then flung them back into place. Waiting behind Jack like a vulture, Ben shoved a few parts into his pockets when Jack finished counting the batch.

"There's no reason my old man should be taking Austin to Nationals in my place," Jack growled, looking for any place to vent his anger.

"If it weren't for you giving him parts, he wouldn't even be racing this year," Ben said, adding fuel to the raging fire that burned inside Jack. "I say he owes you big time."

"And I say we start collecting," Jack said.

Later that afternoon, Cindy showed the

month-end inventory reports to Gary. "This month, inventory loss jumped to nearly thirty-five hundred. Last month it was around twenty-seven," Cindy said.

Ben overheard their conversation and edged closer to them. He didn't want to miss what could be a golden opportunity.

"Are you sure?" Gary asked.

"I went back a year," Cindy said. "It started last September and the loss each month after that gets bigger and bigger."

"What happened in September?" Gary asked.

"You hired Austin," Ben whispered. "Check out his bike. It's got all your missing parts."

Cindy immediately came to his defense. If she had to pick sides between Austin and Ben, it certainly wouldn't be Ben. "He paid for everything," she said flatly as she looked at Gary. He felt the same way about Austin that his wife did.

"Yeah? When did you sell him a set of Pro Tapers?" Ben kept his voice low.

Cindy tried to remember but couldn't.

"Remember that mysterious insurance bill? Didn't Austin break his hand just before you got that bill?" Ben tried not to smile, but he was really enjoying himself. "If I remember right, Jack said something about having his wallet lifted at school."

As far as Gary was concerned, there was

only one way to settle this. "Austin," Gary called across the showroom, "Can I talk to you in my office?"

Cindy went in to the office first, sat behind the desk and folded her arms firmly across her chest. Austin walked in smiling and sat in the chair across from her. Gary followed him in but left the door wide open. Thinking he might be up for another raise, Austin continued to smile.

As soon as they were all in the office, Ben picked up the phone and quickly dialed the local police department. He knew Cindy wouldn't waste any time with small talk.

"Did you pay for the Pro Tapers that are on your bike?" Cindy asked straight out. Austin was caught off guard, but it only took him a second to figure out what was going on.

"No," he said. Austin respected them too much to lie to them.

"Did you use Jack's insurance card when you broke your hand?" Cindy said, rapidly firing the next question.

"Yeah," Austin said and hung his head.

"Do you have an explanation? Anything you want to say?" Gary asked in astonishment.

Austin thought for a second. Even though Jack wasn't a true friend, they had known each other a very long time and his parents had enough to worry about with Amanda's pregnancy. Austin didn't feel that it was his place to tell Gary and Cindy what Jack and Ben were really up to. Austin just shook his head.

"No," he said quietly.

Gary couldn't believe his ears. "There are two things I won't tolerate, Austin. That's a liar and a thief. You're fired!"

Without saying a word Austin stood up and left the office. Walking past Ben and Jack, who quickly scurried away from the office door opening, Austin grabbed his helmet from behind the counter and left through the front door without looking back.

Outside of Coast Range Cycle, Austin strapped on his helmet and pulled his goggles into place. He grabbed the handlebars and started to throw his leg over his bike when he saw the word "user" carved into his seat. Even though it meant buying a new seat, Austin tried to shrug it off. He knew the truth. He hoped that some day Gary would too.

He got on his bike, started it and peeled out of the parking lot onto the city street. At the same moment, a police car pulled out from behind Coast Range Cycle and turned on the police lights. Austin looked back only once to verify he was the target, then gassed it and sped away from the cop.

Austin quickly reached the edge of town where blacktop gave way to gravel road. Traveling too fast, Austin screamed his KTM around a corner and nearly went down in the loose rock. The police lights blinked at him through the dust. Austin quickly recovered and shot straight up the steep road.

The officer, still determined to catch him, watched the bike catch air as it disappeared over the crest of a hill.

As soon as he landed, Austin slowed and darted into the woods on a deer trail. When the police car flew over the hill looking for him, Austin had already vanished.

In the coolness of the woods and on the moist dirt of the deer trail, Austin rode like a speed skater on flawless ice. He glided around trees, rocks and stumps like they weren't even there. His movements were fluid, perfect and beautiful. It would be a terrible waste for the sport of Motocross to lose an athlete with this much raw talent.

Austin pulled his bike into the thick trees at the edge of his overgrown yard, killed the engine and waited in the shadows of the dark woods.

Just as he suspected, the officer pulled up, got out of the police car and knocked on the front door. When no one answered, the officer walked behind the house. Seeing nothing but trash, junk and weeds, the officer headed back to his car.

Just as the officer was ready to pull away, Steve came home and got out of his pickup. Austin watched pensively as his dad talked to the cop. There would be no escape this time. The officer handed Steve a ticket.

After the officer pulled out of the driveway, Austin boldly pushed his bike into his basement shop and waited for the storm. In Austin's mind, he thought he had nothing left to lose. But he was wrong.

When Steve opened the door to the house, the phone was already ringing. Austin listened to the call from the bottom of the stairway.

"Hello?" Steve answered the phone. Steve listened but said nothing. For Austin, the silence was telling.

"Thanks for letting me know." Steve hung up the phone and looked down at the three hundred dollar ticket in his hand.

In the kitchen, Steve fixed a stiff Screwdriver and took a long, slow drink.

Austin slowly wiped the dust off his Regional trophy and wondered how long he would have to wait until his dad came downstairs.

Upstairs Steve slowly and casually fixed another drink. He raised it to his lips then quickly downed the whole thing.

Austin leaned against the workbench and stared at his bike.

Steve fired his empty glass into the sink. Like the starting bell of a boxing match, Austin heard it shatter into a million pieces. It must be time.

Austin watched the garage door roll open as the wheels squeaked out a warning. Steve entered and stood just inside the open door. Like a gunslinger in a showdown, he slowly dropped his hands to his side. Austin looked at him. Here it comes.

But instead of coming straight for him, Steve slowly reached out and picked up a long-handled sledgehammer that was propped next to the door. Now Austin was scared. The adrenaline shot through his body like water through a pressure washer.

In what seemed like one motion to Austin, Steve picked up the sledge with both hands and lunged toward him. But instead of making contact with Austin's body, the hammer landed on the engine of the KTM - right on target. In a violent fury, Steve pummeled the motorcycle over and over and over.

"No! Dad! Stop it! NOT MY BIKE!" Austin screamed at the top of his lungs. Austin rushed toward him and narrowly missed the wrath of the sledge as it made contact with the fuel tank. Pieces flew off. Fuel leaked.

The distinctive smell of gas and two-stroke oil permeated the basement and instantly transported Austin back to racing. Sparked by the unexpected smell, Austin charged toward Steve in a blind fury entirely separate from his father's. Austin loved racing for the life it promised. Steve hated it for the death it represented.

Enraged, Steve took another swing and Austin jumped out of the way just in time. Bingo. The sledge bounced off a destroyed rim.

As Steve raised the sledge up for another strike, Austin timed it better and slammed his head into his dad's gut, knocking him back into the stack of boxes and junk.

The sledge flew out of Steve's hand, sailed through the air and made its final landing on the already destroyed KTM.

Austin climbed on top of Steve and pummeled him with both fists. Steve threw him off, but Austin kept coming back.

Austin's expression said it all. He'd had enough.

Fast-paced and bloody, they continued the brawl until Steve landed a punch on Austin's jaw that sent him reeling into the heap of boxes. The old motocross trophies spun wildly across the dusty concrete floor.

Blood dripping from his mouth, Austin picked himself up, charged Steve again and knocked him backward into the wall. Steve's head slammed hard into the concrete block. He went down with a thud and lay heaped in a semiconscious pile.

"It's over, you bastard!" Austin screamed at him. "I won't watch you destroy my life and my dreams ANYMORE!"

Fading in and out of consciousness, Steve was done. He curled into the fetal position next to Austin's destroyed motorcycle and passed out.

Austin was breathing hard and a bloody mess. As he stared at his father, his anger was replaced by self-disgust. What he feared had happened - he had become his dad.

## Chapter 19 – COURAGE

Sitting in their back booth at Paradise Pizza the following night, Brooke and Austin picked at the pizza in front of them. Austin was glad that the tall seat backs partially hid them from view from the other customers. His face was still bruised and swollen.

"Nationals are still a week away," Brooke said.

"What difference does it make?" Austin stated. "No way to get there, nothing to ride."

"Don't give up, Austin. You only have one life, remember?"

"Why don't you face reality just once?" Austin snapped, completely frustrated.

Brooke was caught off guard by Austin's anger, but rose to the challenge. She was the type of girl that would survive going down with the ship because she had taught herself to swim.

"Because I believe we create our own reality," Brooke fired back. "If you quit, you lose. And what you fear most will become your new reality. You *will* end up like your dad. You know it's all about choice."

"You don't get it, do you?" Austin shook his head.

"There's always a way, Austin. You just have to find it," Brooke said. "And you won't ever find it if you give up."

Just then, Cindy and Gary entered the

restaurant. Unaware that Austin and Brooke were in the back booth, Gary sat down in a booth on the other side of the dining room while Cindy headed for the restroom.

"Be right back," Cindy said to Gary.

When Cindy came out of the restroom, she looked at Brooke as she walked past her, but said nothing. Totally engrossed in his problems, Austin leaned on the table and rubbed his forehead with both hands. He didn't notice Cindy walk by.

A short time later, Jack flung the restaurant door open and stomped inside. All pumped up and looking like a hoodlum, Jack wore his earrings and a muscle shirt that showed off his tatts. Still on crutches, Ben was dressed the same and tried to keep up with him.

Jack strutted up to Austin's table. Austin glanced over at Brooke, who shook her head.

"Don't," she whispered. "Not now."

"What do you want?" Austin asked Jack. "I'm not in the mood for more of your B.S."

"Outside, loser," Jack demanded.

Gary recognized Jack's voice and started to get up, but Cindy grabbed his arm.

"Wait a minute," she said. "We might learn something."

Reluctantly, Gary stayed seated and listened to the heated arguement.

"I'm not gonna fight you, Jack. Your old man may be a millionaire, but you're not worth the effort," Austin said.

Austin's cool demeanor upset Jack even more. He wanted to fight and tried to provoke Austin.

"Screw you!" Jack said. "I knew you added water to your old man's vodka. But that last bottle was the straight stuff!"

"What? That was last fall! You're just figuring that out? What'd you do, wreck your truck?" Austin tried not to grin, but couldn't help it. It would serve Jack right.

Jack grabbed Austin by the jacket, pulled him out of the booth and slammed him against the back of the booth next to Brooke.

"No, it's your fault Amanda's pregnant! Eighty-one thousand dollars? Well, now it's payback time," Jack snapped.

Austin pulled Jack's arm away from his jacket and stepped toward him. After last night, he no longer feared getting his ass kicked. Bring it on. His repressed anger erupted like a volcano. Spit flew into Jack's face as he yelled back.

"Payback for what?" Austin demanded. "I didn't screw Amanda, you did. So now she's screwing you." Austin gave it back to Jack with both barrels.

"We all make mistakes," Austin continued, his voice getting louder with each breath. "Like it was a big mistake trading you my old man's vodka for bike parts, but I figured he was better off without the booze anyway. But, when I started working for Gary, I drew the line. I don't steal from my boss. It's Ben that doesn't have a problem with it and you know it!"

Gary and Cindy quickly exchanged glances.

"I never should have asked you for help when I broke my hand either! Another mistake. Your little insurance scam cost me two more bottles *and* my job!"

Jack didn't back down, so Austin stepped closer and got right in Jack's face. He punched his finger into his chest as he spoke.

"But your mistake Jack?" Austin nailed it home in a voice that demanded to be heard. "It's the biggest one of all. Of all the dads in the entire world, you got the best one! Gary gives you the best bikes, the best equipment, the best of everything! It makes me SICK that you don't appreciate what you've got! Your mistake is not getting Amanda pregnant or blowing off simple maintenance at Regionals – it's being a self-centered, arrogant prick that thinks the world owes you a free ride! WELL SCREW YOU, JACK! One of these days you'll  wake up and it'll all be gone!"

Austin felt his bottled-up rage begin to boil over. He has said enough, maybe too much, and decided to get out of there before things got completely out of control. On his way toward the door, Austin shoved Ben out of his way. "Right, Ben?"

As Ben fell back into a tangle of crutches and chairs, Brooke gathered her things and followed Austin out of the restaurant.

---

After Brooke pulled her VW Bug into Austin's driveway, he got out and led the way through the overgrown weeds to his basement shop.

Inside the door, Austin reached in and flipped the light switch. The fluorescent fixture once again lit up Austin's back corner. What once was a spotless workbench, an organized tool board and swept clean concrete floor, was now a disaster.

Brooke's mouth dropped open when she saw Austin's KTM.

His diamond in the rough was now destroyed. Dented and bent in every conceivable spot, it looked like it had been hit by a log truck. The rest of the garage looked like a tornado had ripped through it.

"This is my reality," Austin said.

"Oh my God," she said. No wonder Austin felt powerless. Brooke stared at the bike then slowly looked around the demolished room in complete shock. When she saw the trophies on the floor, she walked over and picked one up.

"Are these yours?" Brooke asked.

"No," Austin said.

"Who's are they?" she asked.

"I don't know," Austin said. He really didn't know. The trophies had been hidden for over thirty years.

Brooke picked one up and read the plate. "First place. Two fifty CC. Hare Scrambles. 1970." She handed a large one to Austin who wiped dust off the tarnished brass plate.

"Second place. Two hundred mile Enduro. 1970," Austin read. Brooke handed him another. "First place. Washougal. Two fifty CC Moto. 1972." Austin and Brooke were stunned.

"Was your dad a pro?" Brooke asked in surprise.

"I don't know," Austin said, equally surprised. "I know he used to ride a lot, but he won't talk about it."

Steve appeared in the doorway behind Austin and Brooke. His hands were stuffed into the front pockets of his jeans.

"Maybe you should ask him," Brooke said.

"Maybe you should," said Steve quietly.

Startled, Brooke and Austin turned and looked at Steve, who was also beaten and bruised.

"Can we talk?" Steve asked quietly.

"Sure," Austin replied.

"Alone?" Steve said.

Austin turned to Brooke and kissed her. "It'll be okay. I'll call you tomorrow. Thanks for tonight."

After Brooke left, Austin and Steve sat on the front step and listened to the crickets chirp. It was peaceful. For the first time that Austin could remember, Steve didn't have a drink in his hand.

"Dirtbikes scare the hell out of me," Steve said. "Didn't used to. I loved them. When I was your age, everyone told me that I was on my way and should think about turning pro."

Austin looked at Steve's shaking hands, but said nothing. Steve grinned as he remembered his childhood.

"I was good, but so was my younger brother John. Man, we were competitive. We were always trying to beat each other. The harder I pushed, the faster he'd ride." Steve stopped smiling and held his shaking hands tight together.

"But our dad was a real son-of-a-bitch and John suffered the brunt of his anger. I promised myself I'd never be like my dad," Steve's voice cracked. "Now look at me. I'm just like him."

Austin looked at the ground. He knew exactly how he felt.

Steve sucked in a deep breath and continued. "I watched John die during a qualifying race at Washougal," Steve's voice shook as tears streamed down his face. "Dad blamed me for the accident and nearly beat me to death. I never raced again."

"Was it your fault?" Austin had to know.

"I could have stopped John from riding that day, I guess, but I didn't," Steve confessed. "Every night before I fall asleep, I see him die again and again." Steve took a slow breath in and tried to get control over himself.

"Every time I see you ride, I see my brother die." Steve's voice started to crack. "I can't let you die on a bike, Austin," Steve said. "I couldn't take it."

"And I can't live like this. Racing motocross is my dream, Dad," Austin said. "I have to find a way to get to Nationals."

Steve's lips quivered as he failed to fight back the tears that had been fighting their way to the surface since he was Austin's age. Like the release of torrential rain from the blackest of thunderclouds, Steve finally let go and cried. He cried for his dead brother and their abuse, for his lost wife and for Austin. The bitter, sobering reality of what his life had become was painfully clear.

Austin draped his left arm over his Steve's heaving shoulders and watched over his sobbing father as Steve plunged back in time and finally hit his personal rock bottom.

## Chapter 20 – OWNERSHIP

Trying to get to the bottom of the parts scandal, Gary immediately took over the inventory. The next day, he counted every part and piece of inventory on the sales floor, in the shop and in the stock room. Nearing the end of a long day of counting, Gary pulled down Ben's box from the top shelf and looked inside. The box was still half full of dime bags of weed.

"Jack! Get in here," Gary yelled at the top of his voice.

The technicians in the shop stopped working momentarily and looked at each other. They knew this was bound to happen sooner or later. For the sake of their jobs, they were relieved it was sooner.

Jack strolled lazily into the stock room but froze mid-movement the moment he saw Gary holding the box.

"I could lose the business over this!" Gary was furious. He put the box down and got in Jack's face.

"It's not mine," Jack stammered defensively.

"Whose is it?" Gary demanded.

"I don't know," Jack said.

But Gary didn't buy it. He wasn't stupid. Gary jabbed his finger into Jack's chest as he spoke.

"The hell you don't! Answer me!" Gary's

voice boomed.

Jack was instantly subdued and didn't say a word. He didn't know where to start. He had *never* seen his dad this angry before.

"You have one chance," Gary continued, "to redeem yourself or you're through! Take your pregnant girlfriend and get the hell out! I'm not risking everything I've worked for all my life for a few bags of pot!"

"I'll get rid of it," Jack offered, looking for the easy way out.

"No, it's time to grow up, Jack! I want a name or you're finished here forever," Gary said. "Your choice!"

For once, Gary's words hit home. Jack believed him and was afraid of the possibility. Where would he go? What would he do? He had never thought about it before now.

"Okay," Jack said. "Fine."

---

Later that day, Ben slipped in the back stockroom door. Jack tried to avoid him and went back to work on a motorcycle in the shop.

When Jack came back into the stockroom for parts, he heard a faint knock at the back door. He looked around nervously, opened it a crack and peeked through. He nodded then shut the door. "It's for you," Jack whispered to Ben.

Having perfected the use of crutches, Ben made his way to the   inventory shelves at a quick pace. He pulled the box off the shelf and stuffed a handful of dime bags down the front of his pants. He replaced the box then hobbled his way out the back door.

Once Ben left the stockroom, Jack slowly pulled the door closed then leaned against it.

Outside, Ben crutched up to a waiting car with two teenage kids inside. He handed them the pot and took their money. As the car pulled away, Ben went back to the door and tried to open it. But it was locked.

Realizing that Jack was messing with him, Ben grinned and turned around and headed for his truck. No point in hanging around. His deal was done.

Just then, four police cars screeched to a halt and blocked Ben and the teenager's car in. A few minutes later, Gary opened the back door and gave the box of pot to an officer. Jack watched as Ben's hands were handcuffed behind his back and two officers carried Ben by the arms to a waiting patrol car.

Ben glared at Jack from the back seat of the patrol car. He should have figured this would happen. Jack always had, and always would, take the easiest path.

Gary had a million speeches in his mind for Ben, but said nothing. He wasn't worth it. Instead, he walked up to the patrol car and threw Ben's crutches like spears through the patrol car window.

---

Across town, Steve walked into the pawnshop. With violently shaking hands, he took off his gold watch and placed it on the glass counter.

"What will you give me for it?" Steve asked.

Nick looked slightly concerned. "What's going on? You okay?"

"Yeah, I'm fine," Steve said. "Really."

"How much you need?" Nick asked.

"Five hundred?" Steve asked.

Without blinking, Nick tagged the watch. He counted a bundle of twentys then handed the money to Steve.

"Thanks, Nick," Steve said.

"See you later." Shaking his head, Nick watched Steve walk out of the pawnshop.

Steve pulled into the parking lot just as the police car was pulling out. He looked at Ben in the back seat.

Steve stuffed his shaking hands into his pockets and walked up to Gary in the showroom.

"Looks like you've had quite a day," Steve said.

"Yeah," Gary shook his head. "Kids. It doesn't end when they turn eighteen, does it?"

"No, I guess not. Do you have a minute?" Steve asked. He needed his advice and his help.

"Sure," Gary said.

Gary and Steve meandered aimlessly around the showroom floor as they talked. Steve knew that Gary was the only one who knew the whole story.

"I still dream about his death," Steve almost whispered.

"Steve, that was over thirty years ago. Don't you think it's about time you got over it?" Gary wasn't in the mood to be gentle.

"How do you get over killing your own brother?" Steve asked.

"Kill him?" Gary was silent for a moment, as he questioned his own thoughts. "Listen," he finally said. "Everyone knew it was suicide."

"But John told me he was going to do it and I didn't try to stop him," Steve confessed quietly. All these years, he thought he was the only one that knew.

"Well, neither did I. Hell, he said it so often, nobody thought he was serious." Gary said "It's not your fault Steve, anymore than it's mine," Gary continued. "If you need to blame someone, blame your dad."

"Dad said that if I hadn't pushed him to race, he wouldn't have died. I can't do that to Austin." Steve's eyes started to tear up.

"Austin's racing isn't about you. Or your brother. It's about Austin...and his dream," Gary said softly, trying to put it in perspective for Steve.

"But what if...?" Steve questioned the old demons that still haunted him.

Gary stopped walking and faced Steve. He put his hands on both of Steve's shoulders. "That's the funny thing about fear, Steve. The only way out is through."

"I'm not sure what you mean," Steve said.

"You can't run from it," Gary explained. "In order for the fear to go away, you've got to face it. You've got to live through it."

# Chapter 21 –
# CHOOSING THE RIGHT PATH

Two days later, Brooke and Austin pulled into the parking lot of Coast Range Cycle and parked next to Steve's truck.

"What's he doing here?" Austin asked.

Ignoring his question Brooke said, "Bobby's parts are in. I'll be right back."

Brooke walked up to the front door and held it open. A moment later, Steve rolled a brand new KTM SX250 into the parking lot. Grinning ear to ear, Gary followed him out. This was his favorite part of running a motorcycle business.

When Steve waved Austin over, Austin got out of the car in a daze and walked up to the new motorcycle.

"It's for you, son," Steve said.

In disbelief, Austin ran his hand over the tight seat, and looked at Brooke. She smiled and laughed, but said nothing, This wasn't her moment. This was Steve's and Gary's.

Austin walked over to Gary and shook his hand. "Thanks."

Austin turned back to Steve and looked at him. With tears in both their eyes, Austin gave his dad a hug. "Thank you," Austin said.

After Steve let go, Austin jumped on the bike and threw both fists into the air. He yelled, "I'm going to Tennessee!"

Everyone laughed. They didn't notice the taxi that was pulling into the parking lot behind them.

"Come on back tomorrow Austin and we'll get it ready for Nationals," Gary said. "We leave in three days."

"You're coming, right?" Austin asked Steve.

"I'd love to, but there's something I have to do. Gary's got the trip all planned," Steve said. "Give it all you got, Austin. For both of us."

Steve pulled a small duffel bag from his truck then tossed Austin his keys. He waved and got into the cab.

A short time later, Steve got out of the cab and carried his duffel bag into the Inpatient Rehab Center. Steve knew that for all alcoholics, recovery began with the choice to be sober, but he would need help.

---

At the wheel of his luxury motorhome, Gary towed the motorcycle cargo trailer past a huge billboard. The exterior of the trailer was plastered with Coast Range Cycle and KTM decals. The billboard, which marked their final destination and the end to their two thousand mile journey, read "Loretta Lynn's AMA Amateur & Youth Motocross Championship".

Gary turned the air conditioning to high as

he slowed the motorhome to a stop and waited in line at the entrance booth. Even though it was ninety-five degrees outside, Austin couldn't wait to get out of the motorhome and be a part of it. Filled with eager anticipation, he was thrilled by what he saw.

Motocross racers, their families and sponsors inhabited a virtual pop-up city of campers, tents and RVs. Near the track, vendors sold everything from corn dogs and cotton candy to carburetor jets and helmets.

Gleaming semis from every manufacturer and sponsor were present in the sprawling pits. Technicians prepped motorcycles under impressive awnings, each one proudly branded with the company's huge logo. Semi trailers were outfitted as a complete mechanic's shop with all the latest tools or an entire retail store on wheels.

"A little bigger than Washougal isn't it?" Gary grinned, remembering what it felt like when the whole world was brand new. "They'll need your driver's license."

"This is amazing! There must be five thousand people here!" Austin exclaimed as he pulled out his license and his own insurance card from his wallet.

"Right around eight thousand last year," Gary said. "Nationwide, eighteen thousand riders entered the qualifying program but only about thirteen hundred made it to nationals. With five teams represented, only a handful picked up a Factory Ride." Gary pulled up to the booth and rolled down his window. The hot air spilled into the motorhome like heat billowing from a blast furnace.

"How many?" the boot attendant asked.

"Just the two of us," Gary said.

"Rider's name, sponsor and state?" the booth attendant asked.

"Austin Davis. Coast Range Cycle, Oregon," Gary said as he handed him Austin's driver's license and insurance card. Gary filled out a check for the entrance fees and smiled at the attendant. "It's a heck-of-a tax write off and worth every penny."

The attendant smiled back as he punched the information into a keyboard. He knew all about the business side of racing motorcycles. Motocross was exploding in popularity and already a billion-dollar industry. Families spent thousands on it every year.

"You're in space seven forty-five," the attendant said. "Get set up then head for registration."

Gary handed Austin a campground map as he pulled away from the booth. The map looked more like a small city than an RV park.

In the pits, Bill Mitchell opened the rear doors on the Fox  trailer and helped a worker lower a huge set of steps to the ground with a winch and cables. Inside the trailer was an impressive retail display laden with everything that  Fox sold. Ron Heben walked up and shook

Bill's hand.

"Good to see you Bill. How's it going?" Ron asked.

"Great," Bill grinned. "Here to watch the Jack Attack?"

"He didn't qualify," Ron answered. "DNF'd in the last moto at Regionals. Chain flew off."

"That right? Some sort of freak accident?" Bill asked.

"Laziness." Ron continued, "There's a kid from the Northeast region and one from the Southwest that have pretty good track records. And a few newbee's with big dreams. Time will tell."

After finding their RV site and getting the motorhome all hooked up and level, Austin and Gary made their way to the registration desk and stood in the long line that snaked out of the building.

Austin didn't mind waiting. Activity was everywhere. He was completely absorbed by his new surroundings and the time in line gave him a chance to look around. Trying to sneak a peek at the track, Austin wasn't paying attention when Gary grabbed him by the arm and jerked him off the sidewalk and out of the way of two young boys riding by on skateboards. Following them was a herd of kids on BMX bikes.

"We'll take a look at it later," Gary grinned as he nodded toward the track.

An hour later, the booth worker called

"Next!"

Austin and Gary stepped up to the window.

The worker spoke quickly and handed Austin his transponder and mounting strips. "The transponder must be taped to the top or back of your helmet with these," the worker said. "Make sure your helmet is free of dirt or oil before you attach it. Keep it in your possession at all times and don't get it mixed up with anyone else's."

"Lap times," Gary explained to Austin. "It's all computerized."

"You must have a transponder on your helmet anytime you are on the track," the worker continued. "They'll be removed after the third moto as the riders exit the track. If you don't complete the third moto, turn it in before you leave the facility. Here is the race schedule, park rules, map and events calendar. What class?" the worker asked.

"Two-fifty Open A," Austin replied.

The worker grabbed a number set from the stack and handed them to Austin.

"Be sure your numbers are mounted on each of your bike's three numberplates and on both sides of your helmet. Next!"

Austin looked at his number as he and Gary left the registration building.

"What number you get?" Gary asked.

Austin held up his numbers.

"Seventy-nine," Austin said.

Looking like he'd just seen a ghost, Gary

turned pale and swallowed hard. He hoped this wasn't a sign of bad things to come.

"What's wrong?" Austin asked. "You okay?"

"Must be the heat," Gary said.

It was the first week of August and the southern Tennessee sky stayed light well into the evening. Wanting to know what he would be up against in tomorrow's race, Austin walked the track with Gary and scrutinized every detail in dazed silence. In the long evening shadows of a large pine tree that grew right next to the track, they stopped and studied a tight corner.

"We both know your weak area is really sharp corners," Gary said as he pointed to the track. "I'd suggest riding a line close to the inside. It will give you more room for error in case something happens."

Austin considered Gary's suggestion then asked, "What about taking the outside and using the berm?"

"If you overshoot the turn on that line, you'll hit the berm head on," Gary answered as he gestured an abrupt arc depicting the movement of the bike, "and get launched. Geometry and physics will see to it."

# Chapter 22 – CONFRONTATION

That night, Austin went to bed in Tennessee for the first time in his life. That same night, also for the first time in his life, Steve asked for help.

"Hi. My name is Steve."

"Hi Steve," a chorus of injured souls with comforting voices greeted him. Steve looked at the faces in the circle of recovering alcoholics.

"I'm here," Steve paused, "because I love my son."

---

The following morning was Tuesday and a huge crowd of families, supporters and industry professionals gathered in the grandstands and around the Loretta Lynn Motocross track to watch the races that were scheduled to run all day long.

In mid-afternoon, the hottest part of the day, the 250 class pulled up to the line for their first moto. Their second moto was scheduled for Thursday and the final 250 moto, which was the premier event of Nationals, was scheduled for Saturday.

Austin rode his new bike up to the starting gate and mentally thanked his dad for the gift. He was grateful he wasn't trying to compete on his old bike. Stuck in the middle of the line, Austin looked both ways at his competitors.

Each kid was a complete stranger, wore brand new gear and rode a new bike. Honda's, Kawasaki's, Yamaha's, Suzuki's and KTM's were all equally represented. Austin dropped his head, said his words and waited.

When the gates dropped, the pack escaped into the race. Austin pulled out of the first corner in fourth position and attacked the course with every bit of strength and every ounce of determination he had. Even though the track was watered, the race was hot, dusty and grueling. And his competition was fast! Austin only managed to pass one rider by the end of the race. The importance of making the holeshot took on a whole new meaning here.

Ron was standing next to the track when Austin flew across the finish line in third place. Maybe this kid had something more than just big dreams. Ron made a mental note to keep his eye on him.

At the end of the day, Austin and Gary waited for the crowd to thin then found his name and confirmed his third place finish on the monitors. One down, two motos to go.

As they were walking back to the motorhome, Austin looked out over the thousands of campers and kids.

"Gary, honestly, what do you think my chances are for picking up a Factory Ride?" Austin asked.

Gary thought for a moment before speaking. "The odds are long, but it happens every year," he said. "Try not to get ahead of yourself, Austin. Take each race one at a time. I opened a motorcycle business because I love motorcycles, not because I wanted to be named Business Man Of The Year or make a ton of money. Those things happened because I love what I do. Do you love racing?"

"Yeah, I love riding."

"That's different than racing. You gotta love the crowds, the training, the traveling, the adrenaline, the thrill of winning, and the opportunities of losing. That will be your *job* if you get a Factory Ride."

"I never thought of it like that," Austin said.

"When riders imagine themselves as a Factory Rider, most of them envision signing autographs and having their picture in all the magazines. Because they focus on the wrong goal, they never make it. If you focus on the job of racing, you'll do fine."

"But sometimes I get so nervous. Especially here."

"Try singing to yourself. Something silly. It works for me."

Austin looked at Gary and smiled. They walked for a while in silence. The temperature was finally starting to drop. As it cooled off, the atmosphere and energy in the camps seemed to relax and slow down as well.

"I'm going to that get-together tonight with the other motorcycles dealers," Gary said as he tossed him the keys. "Will you be okay by yourself for an hour or two?"

"Of course. Besides, I need to clean up my bike," Austin replied. "See you later."

Austin went back to their campsite, took his bike out of the trailer and started to clean it. Carefully scrutinizing each part, he looked for anything that could possibly go wrong.

As Austin slid a piece of film negative into the front fork seals, another rider walked by carrying a basketball and stopped to watch Austin work on his bike.

"Trouble?" the rider asked.

Austin looked up and recognized him immediately. "Umm, no, just getting the grit out of the seals," Austin said.

"Show me what you do." The rider dropped his basketball on the ground and sat on it, only inches from Austin's front wheel.

"You're James Stewart, right, the best rider in the 125 class in the entire United States?"

"Yeah, but don't tell anyone," he teased. "How does it work?" James nodded toward Austin's front fork.

Proud that his bike was new and in perfect condition, Austin carefully slid the film into the other fork seal, moved it carefully around the seal, then gently pulled it out. "Keeps 'em from leaking. They last longer." Austin held the film up to the light. It was covered with particles of grit and dust.

"Cool!" James exclaimed. "Got any

extra?"

"Sure," Austin said.

Austin handed James a fresh film negative from an envelope inside his toolbox.

"Are you riding?" Austin asked.

"It's a promotional deal," James replied as he stood and picked up his basketball. "Thanks for the film. Hey, you got time for a break? Play some ball?"

Austin hesitated. He came here to race, not screw around and socialize. The pro sensed his uneasiness.

"I'll trade you tips," James coached. "You'll ride better if you relax between races. C'mon."

On his way back to the camp, Gary walked by the Loretta Lynn Arena and grinned as he watched Austin play basketball with the group of famous pro riders. Laughing and having a blast, they acted like they had known each other for years.

For the first time in his life, Austin felt like he fit in.

---

In the second Moto on Thursday, Austin had a better feel for the track. Even though he was in fourth place coming out of the corner, he was able to pass all but one of the riders ahead of him and take second place.

After it was over, Gary and Austin walked

up the scoreboard to check the monitors. The group of Honda scouts was just leaving.

Gary heard one of the scouts talking about "that Davis kid" as they walked past them and wondered what was going on. Gary looked up at the monitor and smiled. Following Austin's last name was a "two" under the Moto two column. Austin was tied for second place overall!

Austin realized that James' advice about relaxing between races was right on.

That afternoon, when it was pushing ninety-eight degrees, Austin beat the heat and cooled off with a group of riders. One at a time, they took turns jumping off the hot rocks of the cliffs into the cool, deep and refreshing river that ran past the edge of the campground. The dust and the stress of racing were washed away with the current as Austin swam back to the side of the river and climbed out.

Back in Oregon, washing away years of alcoholism was not so easy. Starting to go through withdrawals, Steve rocked back and forth on his bed inside a small, sparsely furnished room at the rehab center. Gary's words played over and over in his mind. "*The only way out is through.*" But, Steve wasn't sure he could make it to the other side.

On Saturday, a huge crowd gathered around the Loretta Lynn Track for the last race. As the premier event of Nationals, it would help the scouts determine which riders they would consider for the elusive Factory Ride.

Close to the inside, and with more riders to his right than his left, Austin crouched down on his bike at the starting gate. The first corner was a straight shot.

"My choice. My way," Austin said., "And my win."

As soon as the gate dropped, Austin bolted off the line and flat out flew into the corner. Relaxed and ready, Austin made it look easy. He maneuvered his bike with perfection and shot through the pack unscathed. The holeshot was his!

Increasing his lead, Austin rode the track like the pro he knew he could be. Bike engines roared. Riders went down. Dirt flew. The huge crowd that was gathered along the track roared and cheered vociferously.

Back in Oregon, the noise inside Steve's head was equally deafening. Lying on his bed in the rehab center, he flashed back once again to that horrific motocross race.

In the same yellow haze, Steve saw the 70's motocross rider dressed in all black, speed recklessly away from him. Just like before, the Black Rider headed into the corner toward the fir trees grew dangerously close to the track. Suddenly, the bike slammed into the berm head on and pitched the rider into the air. The bike's numberplate was 179.

In the mirror image of Steve's hallucinations, Austin sped toward the corner that he and Gary looked at earlier in the week.

Because of so many races, the once smooth
track was now rutted, and staying on his chosen
line was difficult.

Still riding balls-out, Austin put his left
foot down to stabilize the bike and leaned hard
into the turn. But his boot caught the dirt and
pitched his back wheel to the right then left,
which caused him to lose control. Propelled
forward by the momentum, his bike headed
straight for the berm and slammed head-on into
the dirt. The sudden stop catapulted Austin over
the handlebars, and the berm, then flung him
toward the pine tree.

In his mind, Steve watched in slow motion
as the Black Rider hit the jagged limb on the fir
tree straight on. The body, now violently
skewered to the tree, twitched and jerked as it
tried to escape the pain. Blood spurted from the
wound and dripped off the splintered wood that
protruded through the back of the black jersey.
The rider's head, still protected by the old black
helmet, bobbed against the branch.

"Noooo!" Steve screamed at the nurses.

At that exact moment, Austin flew through
the air, slammed head first into the pine tree and
dropped to the ground with a thud.

Running toward the rider trapped in his
mind, Steve's arms and legs flailed violently in
rehab. Four nurses struggled to hold him down
while another nurse quickly injected a strong
sedative into the I.V. Within seconds, the
sedative took effect.

As Steve's movements slowed, tears welled in his vacant eyes and his labored breathing suddenly ceased. Bouncing in and out of reality, Steve could scarcely breathe as he removed his brother's body from the limb.

With the wind knocked out of him, Austin pulled his smashed goggles over his broken visor and fought for a single breath. While he was on the ground, a rider passed him and sprayed his naked face with dirt kicked up by the knobby tires. An official ran over to Austin to check for injuries.

Slowly, Steve's body stopped twitching and his breathing returned to normal. The nurses took his vital signs then covered his relaxed body with a blanket. By letting the nightmare play out for the first time since his brother's death, Steve was finally able to say goodbye.

After precious seconds ticked away, Austin sucked in a huge breath and got up. Like a madman, he rushed back to his still-running bike, got on and took off. Lost in the heat of the moment, and with dirt still in his eyes, Austin cut the corner tight and got back on the track.

Riding once again without goggles, Austin passed rider after rider until there were only two riders left in front of him.

The crowd went crazy.

Completely absorbed, Ron watched Austin pass the second rider.

One down, one to go. The checkered flags waved ahead.

"C'mon." Ron shook his fist discreetly at his side.

The people left in the pits stopped working and looked toward the loud screaming crowd. People ran to the track to catch the tail-end of the excitement.

Teeth clenched and with all he had, Austin pinned the throttle and leaned into it. He wasn't about to give up now. With only fifty yards to the finish line, he was gaining on the last rider ahead of him. At twenty-five yards to go, his front wheel had passed the other rider's back wheel. At ten yards, they were even.

Austin crossed the finish line just inches ahead of his competitor. First place in the 250cc open class at Nationals was Austin's!

With a wide grin on his face, Ron shook his head in amazement. *That* was racing.

Breathing hard, Austin pulled off the track into the flagged-off area. His face was covered with dust and mud. A worker took the transponder off his helmet.

"Tough break, kid," the worker said. "It was a heck of a race though."

"What?" Austin asked.

"Next!" the worker yelled.

With other riders waiting behind him, Austin rode away and looked back at the worker. "What did that mean?"

## Chapter 23 – REWARDS

The America Motorcycle Association President, a rotund and jovial man, stood behind a podium on the side of the stage. A big plastic banner boasting the AMA Amateur National Champions hung on the wall behind the stage.

"Is this the world's greatest motocross vacation or what?" the AMA President asked the cheering crowd.

The crowd cheered louder. Ron and Bill stood together near the edge of the crowd and smiled.

"What a week it's been!" the AMA President continued. "Since 1982, Loretta Lynn and her family and the surrounding community here at Hurricane Mills, Tennessee have welcomed thousands of motocross racers, their families and sponsors. As president of the AMA, I'd like to say thanks to all of you who made this year's event another success!"

The crowd applauded and cheered loudly.

"And now," said the president, "I present this year's top riders!"

Ten riders, each from a different riding class and dressed in clean motocross attire, walked onto the stage and held up huge trophies. The crowd cheered.

Austin and Gary watched from the crowd below as photographers snapped pictures of the top ten. Austin dropped his head and looked at the ground. Totally disgusted with himself, he couldn't believe he had made such a big mistake. In fact, he didn't even remember it. The official said he cut the course after wrecking in the third moto and had disqualified him.

After the top ten left the stage, the president continued. "Each year we give out a unique award that symbolizes the events at that year's Nationals. This year, we witnessed fantastic riding and excellent sportsmanship. But, above all, we saw raw desire and unprecedented dedication."

Ron waited and watched for the crowd's response.

"This year the award for outstanding dedication to the sport of Motocross goes to Austin Davis, number seventy-nine!"

Austin's jaw dropped. He was stunned. This was totally unexpected.

"Get up there," Gary nudged Austin. "Act like the pro you want to be. Go on."

Ron watched Austin as he hopped up on the stage and leaned into the microphone.

"Hi. I'm Austin Davis."

The crowd cheered and clapped. Ron and Bill paid close attention. Along with being incredible riders, sponsored kids needed a good public image and the ability to speak comfortably in front of a crowd.

"I'd like to say thanks to everyone who made this week so much fun!" Austin smiled. "I gave it my best shot and rode my best race so far. Having my eyes packed full of dirt was a tough break, but I don't have any hard feelings. I think I'll invest in some new goggles, though. Thank you!"

The crowd laughed and clapped. Gary, Ron and Bill grinned and applauded as Austin left the stage.

"That Austin is quite a kid," said Bill.

---

Packed up and ready to head west in the motorhome, Austin put the last lawn chair inside the cargo trailer and waited for Gary to lock the door.

Ron, carrying his organizer and palm pilot, walked up to them and handed Austin a brand new pair of expensive Spy goggles. "Thought these might come in handy later."

"Wow, thank you," Austin said. He was surprised to see Ron. Because Austin was disqualified in the last moto, he didn't even make the top ten in the 250 class.

"How old are you, Austin?" Ron asked.

"Eighteen," Austin replied.

Austin looked at Gary, who was smiling, then looked back at Ron.

"I've been going over your race data from here and from Regionals," Ron said. "You're a pretty decent rider. No guarantees, but we'd like to fly you out to California for a few days and see what you can do."

"Really?" Austin tried to act professional, but could barely contain his excitement. "Awesome!"

"We'll provide a test bike and all the equipment. We'd like to assess your riding ability and technique, run some physical tests, maybe go over the PR end of it," Ron said as he opened up his organizer. "Two weeks from now, okay?" I'll have a plane ticket sent to your house along with an information packet."

Austin looked at Gary, who nodded and smiled.

"Yeah, sure!" Austin's enthusiasm was overflowing. "I'll be there. Thank you!"

## Chapter 24 – FREEDOM

After three long days on the road, Gary pulled the motorhome into the dark and deserted parking lot of Coast Range Cycle. Brooke's car was the only one on the lot. As soon as they drove up, she got out and waved at Austin.

Before the motorhome even came to a stop, Austin opened the door and jumped out. He ran over to Brooke, picked her up and twirled her in circles.

The following morning, Brooke drove Austin to his dad's house. "Have you told your dad yet?" Brooke asked.

"Not yet," Austin said. "I think he's still in rehab."

With less than a mile to go, a pickup truck with a refrigerator loaded in the back passed them going the opposite direction and caught Austin's eye. When he turned around to look at it, he instantly recognized the avocado green color.

"That's our refrigerator!" Austin gasped.

Then the realization hit him. He slowly turned back around and stared out his passenger window.

"I guess he's done with rehab," Austin muttered.

Brooke pulled her Bug into Austin's driveway and parked next to an unfamiliar car. They watched as a man carried out Steve's TV and put it into his car trunk. A woman walked out behind the man carrying the VCR.

Devastated and disappointed, Austin watched the cars leave. As soon as the car was out of sight, Austin and Brooke slowly got out of her car.

Inside the open front doorway, Austin stood motionless and watched Steve sweep the floor where the refrigerator used to be. The house was clean for once, but the microwave and Steve's watch were still missing.

"Hey Dad," Austin said quietly.

Steve spun around, dropped the broom and ran over to Austin. With a huge smile on his face, Steve threw his arms around Austin and gave him a hug.

"Congratulations! You got your shot," Steve said.

Austin looked at Brooke as he weakly patted Steve's back. Brooke shrugged her shoulders and discreetly shook her head. Neither one of them knew what to make of Steve's enthusiastic behavior, especially since he was still selling off the household appliances.

"Thanks," Austin said.

Steve let go of Austin and walked over to Brooke. He wasn't sure if he should shake her hand or give her a hug. He decided on the shake and took Brooke's hand.

"Thanks for taking care of him," Steve said.

After Steve dropped Brooke's hand, she

gave him a quick, awkward hug.

"You're welcome," Brooke said. "I'll see you later tonight Austin. Bye, Steve."

Austin closed the door behind Brooke. "What are you doing?" Austin demanded quietly.

"What do you mean?" Steve asked sheepishly.

"The refrigerator? The TV and VCR?" Austin said sarcastically.

Steve picked up the broom and started sweeping again. It took him a second to find the words. "I quit my job when I finished rehab," Steve said. "I started at Alloy Fabricators last week. Being sober and working at the old place just didn't fit. I've got AA every night."

"How did you know about KTM?" Austin asked.

"Gary called from Tennessee," Steve said. "He wanted to run things by me. See how I was doing."

"We're all glad you're getting better." Austin said sincerely.

Steve stopped sweeping and looked directly at Austin.

"Look, Austin, I know I've been a shitty father. I want you to have everything you need for your trip. I want you to make it."

Steve picked up an envelope on the counter and held it out at Austin. "The money is for you."

# Chapter 25 – EDUCATION

Two weeks later, Austin was on his way to California. He bounced in the seat of the huge 747 aircraft during its very rough landing. "This is awesome!" Austin said as he smiled at the passenger in the next seat.

The old man next to him was pale with fear. He gripped the armrests and hung on for dear life. Austin laughed as he visualized the old man trying to ride a dirtbike at full speed.

"Welcome to San Diego," the flight attendant said into the plane's intercom.

Late that afternoon, Austin got out of a cab in Temecula, California and looked up in awe at the brand new KTM Office and Training Center. A cross between a high-rise and a sports arena, this building was the epitome of success in any industry.

Austin felt tiny in comparison as he opened up the heavy glass front door and walked in. Dressed in the best new clothes he could afford, he carried a legal sized manila envelope full of paperwork and waited for Ron in the reception area. Within a few minutes of being called, Ron met Austin and shook his hand.

Seeing a familiar face eased Austin's nervousness. He knew this was his only chance and he didn't want to blow it.

Ron could tell Austin was nervous, but being able to relax under stressful conditions was an important part of racing. The kid would either do well or he wouldn't. For Ron, trying to select the next motocross star out of thousands of riders was an everyday part of business.

As they walked through a maze of corridors, Austin paid careful attention to Ron and answered his interview questions honestly and openly. The process reminded him of working the showroom floor, but Austin was acutely aware that he was selling himself instead of a bike.

"How was your trip?" Ron asked. "The hotel okay? Any problems?"

"Everything's perfect. Thanks," Austin smiled. "Flying was a blast."

"Your first time in a jet?" Ron was surprised. Then he remembered Austin's background and home life.

"Yeah," Austin answered. "It was cool."

Ron motioned to the envelope that Austin carried.

"Birth certificate, medical records and transcripts?" Ron asked. "How'd you do in school?"

Austin nodded and handed him the envelope. "Three point nine."

"What was your favorite class?" Ron continued the informal interview. He opened a door that lead down a long hallway. It smelled like fresh paint and floor wax.

"Physics. Then mechanical engineering," Austin said. "I like to know why things work they way they do."

"That's good. It's important. Most people won't make a team and need to have other options." Ron thought it was best to be candid with the kids from the very beginning.

"Yeah. I know," Austin said. He did know. In the grand scheme of it all, he was amazed that he had made it this far. It's one thing to have a dream, but it's another thing entirely when you get to live it. Even part of it.

"Everyone fails at something," Ron said matter-of-factly. "We tell the young riders to spread out, get a good education and develop their other skills. We tell everyone that there is only a slim chance they will get a Factory Ride."

Ron opened the door that led to KTM's brand new gargantuan indoor arena. Complete with a huge, perfectly groomed Supercross track, electronic video surveillance and time-keeping equipment, this place was state of the art.

Austin was overwhelmed by what he saw. Talk about having the right tools and equipment! The smell of fresh dirt and exhaust instantly started the flow of adrenaline.

Ron and Austin walked up to a team of KTM trainers and technicians that waited just for Austin. "This is your support team," Ron said. "They've been hand-selected to work with you while you're here."

"Wow." Austin grinned and shook hands

with all of them.

"They'll be helping you with on-track analysis and training," Ron said. "Thanks guys. Be back later."

Austin and Ron walked around the perimeter of the arena and continued the interview. "Do you have a girlfriend?" Ron asked.

"Brooke," Austin answered, "but she's in school for one more year."

"Girlfriends are either a great support or a complete distraction," Ron was serious. "They can easily take a rider down. I see it all the time. A kid gets his first factory ride but the girlfriend is all about the glamour and excitement of it all and keeps her boyfriend from practicing and putting in the time and the work."

"I wouldn't have made it to Nationals without her." Austin knew Brooke and how he felt about her. Choosing between her and motocross would be impossible. He hoped it didn't come to that.

Ron opened the door to the Training and Testing Room and flipped on the light switch. Austin looks inside. It was a cross between a doctor's office and a weight room.

"No alcohol, drugs, visible tats or wild piercings," Ron said. "You'll be asked to submit voluntary urine samples at random intervals. Any problem with that?"

"Nope," Austin hesitated, "But, um, well, can I still eat poppyseed muffins?"

"Muffins? Yeah, sure." Ron said.

They continued down the hall until Ron opened another door that was labeled PR Studio. Complete with elaborate recording equipment, it looked like it could be part of a television newsroom - except for the motorcycle on the mock winner's platform and walls that were draped with motocross banners and product insignia.

"This is the PR room. We'll see how you look on camera and give you a few pointers on impromptu acceptance speeches," Ron said.

Austin grinned as he thought back to Nationals. He didn't remember exactly what he said, but realized he must have sounded ridiculous.

"Just one more thing." Ron's tone of voice was serious. When Austin looked at him, a huge smile spread across Ron's face. "Relax," he said. "Have fun while you're here. There's nothing worse than a job that's not any fun!"

The next morning, Austin began his evaluation and training. His emotions darted back and forth between the thrill of actually being there and the fear of screwing up. To help himself relax, he followed Gary's advice and played his favorite song over and over in his head. Occasionally, when no one was listening, he'd sing the words out loud. "Flinstones. Meet the Flinstones..."

Fast paced and tightly scheduled, the next two days passed in a blur.

The team of technicians watched Austin carefully as he rode a test bike on the Supercross track. Video crews filmed his every move and captured his image from two separate angles. When Austin almost lost it in a corner, the trainers stopped the ride immediately.

After everyone watched Austin's errors on video, the trainers explained proper cornering technique. Austin listened carefully, got back on the bike and sailed through the corner perfectly. Being able to actually see what he did wrong made all the difference.

In the Physical Testing Facility, lab techs attached electrodes to Austin's bare chest. His impressive chest muscles flexed as they pressed the circular patches into his skin. Wearing only shorts and running shoes, Austin ran on the treadmill as the electrodes recorded the electrical impulses and his heart rate.

"You're in good shape. Your level of physical conditioning exceeds our standard. Keep up the good work," the lab technician told him.

After he finished the conditioning tests, the lab tech drew blood for the blood work and the drug test. After that, Austin provided a urine sample to complete the tests.

Back on the Supercross track, Austin flew over whoops as an electronic clock displayed his lap time – 68, 69, 70.

In the PR room, the video crew filmed Austin, dressed in new motocross gear, as he gave a mock speech on the fake winner's platform. By this time, Austin was relaxed.

"Most of all I'd like to thank the school cafeteria," Austin chuckled. "Purina is a great sponsor." The video crew laughed. Along with everything else, Austin tried hard to keep in touch with his sense of humor and have fun.

Back on the Supercross track, Austin flew over the whoops as the electronic clock displayed his much faster time – 57, 58, 59.

---

Holding a new KTM duffel bag in his left hand and wearing a bright orange KTM t-shirt, Austin shook Ron's hand as they stood next to a waiting cab.

"We'll let you know in about two weeks after we've had a chance to go over everything," Ron said. "I'll call you on the fifteenth."

"Great. Thanks for everything, Ron," Austin said. "I had a blast."

## Chapter 26 – DESTINY

Still wearing the KTM t-shirt, Austin got out of the cab and walked up the sidewalk to a tidy house in the middle of a suburban San Diego neighborhood. Austin rang the door bell and waited anxiously on the doorstep. Finally, an attractive woman opened the door. She smiled big then hugged him tight.

"Hi, Mom," Austin said as he held her.

"Looks like you found your way," she said. "Come on in."

---

Two weeks later, Jack stood next to Amanda behind the service counter at Coast Range Cycle.

"Hey, Jack. Catch," Gary said.

Jack turned around and looked at his dad. Gary was dressed in full motocross gear and tossed Jack a set of keys. Jack caught the keys then turned back around to Amanda and looked in awe at his brand new baby. A son.

"Thanks, Grandpa," Jack said just as Gary opened the front door to leave.

"Grandpa?" Gary laughed out loud and grinned. That would take a few days to get used to.

---

That same afternoon, Brooke picked

Austin up from Portland International Airport and drove him to his house. When they arrived, they noticed that the yard had been cleaned up considerably and that the house was in the middle of getting a fresh coat of light blue paint.

Carrying his KTM bag and still wearing the KTM t-shirt, Austin walked up to the front door and opened it for Brooke. There was an envelope taped to the door with his name on it. Austin peeled off the envelope and followed Brooke inside. The house was quiet and felt deserted. The microwave, refrigerator, and TV/VCR were still missing.

"Dad?" Austin called out. No answer. Austin walked down the hall.

"He's not here," Austin said to Brooke. "What day is it?"

"Sunday," she said.

Austin opened the envelope. He pulled out a note, a pawn ticket and Polaroid picture of his dad's watch. Austin shuffled nervously as he read the note out loud. He looked distraught, like someone at a funeral.

"Sorry to hear about your dad. To claim the watch, bring the pawn ticket and six hundred dollars to the shop. Good luck, Nick."

"What does that mean?" Brooke asked.

Austin slowly handed the note to Brooke. He couldn't believe it. "Dad's dead?" Austin asked in disbelief. He looked at Brooke, who was also stunned, then looked back at the picture in shock.

Just then, Austin heard motorcycle engines outside. He rushed to the front door and flung it open. Austin and Brooke watched two riders dressed in full motocross gear get off dirtbikes. Slowly, the riders removed their goggles and helmets.

Laughing like teenagers, Gary and Steve walked up to the house.

"Don't worry. We'll take it easy until you get used to it again," Gary told Steve.

"Hey, you're back!" Steve said as soon as he realized Austin was standing in the doorway. He gave him a big hug. "How'd you do?"

Austin watched Steve walk to the sink, fill two glasses with water and hand one to Gary. "Okay, I think," Austin stammered, still dazed and reeling. "Ron said he'd call today with my results."

Gary and Steve downed their water and put the glasses into the clean sink.

"I think this is for you," Austin said as he handed the envelope to Steve.

"What's this?" Steve asked as he read the note and looked at the Polaroid. He looked at Austin and slowly ripped the Polaroid, the pawn ticket and the note in half. "The watch was my dads," Steve said. "Sometimes...when you're trying to find your way...some things are better left behind."

The phone rang once. Austin looked at everyone while it rang two, three and four times. Finally, he answered it.

"Hello?" Austin said, pausing while the caller spoke. "Speaking." Another pause. "Hey, Ron. How are you?"

Brooke clasped her hands together in front of her mouth like she was praying. She looked at Steve and Gary then nodded toward the phone.

"This is it? This is the call?" Steve asked.

Austin nodded then listened intently to the phone call. The expression on his face was serious. All business. "Okay. Fine," Austin said into the phone. "Thanks for calling." Austin hung up the phone and dropped his head.

"Well?" Brooke, Gary and Steve all asked in unison.

Austin took a deep breath and calmly stuffed both fists into his pockets. His eyes welled up with tears and spilled onto his cheeks as he looked at them. Very quietly he said, "I got my Factory Ride." He had waited his whole life to say those words.

Everyone cheered and rushed Austin with hugs and slaps on the back. After the din died down, Steve pulled Austin aside. Gary took the cue and walked outside with Brooke to show off Steve's new bike.

"I'm so proud of you," Steve told Austin. "Congratulations."

"Thanks," Austin said, wiping his eyes. After a short pause he asked, "How are you doing?"

"Forty-two days so far," Steve said. "Some

are better than others. I think riding again will help."

Austin nodded in agreement. He couldn't imagine his life without bikes. It was a form of therapy for him. Hopefully for his dad, too. Steve put his hand on Austin's shoulder.

"I love you, Austin."

Austin looked long and intently into Steve's serious eyes. Slowly, like the lifting of a heavy fog, Austin smiled at his father. Everything was going to be fine.

"Thanks," Austin said sincerely.

They walked outside and joined Gary and Brooke.

"Ready?" Gary asked Steve.

Steve looked at Austin, who waved him on with a grin. "Go. Have a blast," Austin said.

Austin wrapped his arm around Brooke and squeezed her shoulder. "And sometimes," Austin said to Brooke, "it's impossible to leave treasures behind."

"Ready," Steve said.

Arm in arm, Brooke and Austin watched as Steve and Gary got on their bikes and pulled on their helmets.

Steve and Gary grinned at each other then slid their goggles into place. Gary nodded at Steve. Steve nodded back - then flipped him off.

**The End.**

## SCRATCHY HOME MOVIES MEMORIES

A small boy, who could be from a Norman Rockwell painting, bursts into the room on Christmas morning. Next to the tree is a shiny new 1965 Honda 50 motorcycle. The stunned little boy looks at his smiling parents and grins ear to ear. He just got the best present on earth.

On a hot summer day, two boys wearing only helmets, shorts and converse high-tops, race each other through a cow pasture on old XR75's. One of them wrecks and lands in a cow pie. The other boy circles back and laughs.

A teenager sails over a jump in a motocross race on a 1972 CZ. He is lucky to get a foot of air, bottoms out the suspension when he lands, then gasses it and takes off.

A group of men ride late 1970's motorcycles, a Maico, Bultaco, Husquvarna and an Ossa, on wooded trails. They wear open-faced helmets, old-fashioned goggles and gear.

With friends gathered around a man blows out the number five and the number zero on his 50th birthday cake then closes his eyes and makes a wish. His wife gives his shoulders a squeeze as his son rolls out a new dirtbike.

Having just finished a race, men in their sixties and seventies pull off their goggles and smile for the camera beside their vintage motorcycles.